# SHEDDING EGYPT, BECOMING ISRAEL

# *Shedding Egypt, Becoming Israel*

### A Critical Evaluation of Egyptian Culture and Circumcision on the Formation of National Israel

## JOSHUA SETH HOUSTON

*Foreword by* RANDALL C. BAILEY

WIPF & STOCK · Eugene, Oregon

SHEDDING EGYPT, BECOMING ISRAEL
A Critical Evaluation of Egyptian Culture and Circumcision on the Formation of National Israel

Copyright © 2025 Joshua Seth Houston. All rights reserved. Except for brief quotations in critical publications or reviews, no part of this book may be reproduced in any manner without prior written permission from the publisher. Write: Permissions, Wipf and Stock Publishers, 199 W. 8th Ave., Suite 3, Eugene, OR 97401.

Wipf & Stock
An Imprint of Wipf and Stock Publishers
199 W. 8th Ave., Suite 3
Eugene, OR 97401

www.wipfandstock.com

PAPERBACK ISBN: 979-8-3852-4015-9
HARDCOVER ISBN: 979-8-3852-4016-6
EBOOK ISBN: 979-8-3852-4017-3

Scripture quoted by permission. Quotations designated (NET) are from the NET Bible® copyright ©1996, 2019 by Biblical Studies Press, L.L.C. http://netbible.com All rights reserved.

To my wife, Kayla, and to my daughter, Emery.

# Contents

*List of Illustrations and Tables  ix*
*Foreword  xi*
*Preface  xv*
*Acknowledgements  xvii*
*List of Abbreviations  xix*

1: Introduction to the Issues  1
2: The Influence of Egypt on Israel's Secular Mores  22
3: The Influence of Egypt on Israel's Religious Mores  49
4: Was Moses *Really* an Egyptian? The Sources Weigh In  65
5: Becoming Israelite: Joshua 5:2–9 as the Final Stage of Shedding Egyptian Mores  97
6: Conclusion  124

*Bibliography  129*

# List of Illustrations and Tables

Figure 1: Diagram of the Relationship of Now-Actions to Plot
Table 1: English Renderings of *lō'-mālû*
Table 2: A Comparison of Egyptian Mores and the Law of Moses

# Foreword

ABOUT ONE YEAR PRIOR to Isaac's birth, God appeared to Abraham and commanded that all his male descendants should be circumcised on the eighth day following their birth.

> You shall circumcise the flesh of your foreskins, and it shall be a sign of the covenant between me and you. Throughout your generations every male among you shall be circumcised when he is eight days old, including the slave born in your house and the one bought with your money from any foreigner who is not of your offspring. Both the slave born in your house and the one bought with your money must be circumcised. So shall my covenant be in your flesh an everlasting covenant. (Gen 17:11–13 NRSV)

This law continued into the Torah.

> The LORD spoke to Moses, saying: Speak to the people of Israel, saying: If a woman conceives and bears a male child, she shall be ceremonially unclean seven days; as at the time of her menstruation, she shall be unclean. On the eighth day the flesh of his foreskin shall be circumcised. (Lev 12:1 NRSV)

Most students of the Bible have heard from their youth that this act was a "sign" of the covenant, if not one of the most significant signs of God's covenants with Abraham and eventually with the nation of Israel. These facts, when coupled with the esteem given to Moses by God in the Torah and through the biblical corpus, creates a conundrum for the reader of Josh 5:2–5.

> At that time the LORD said to Joshua, "Make flint knives and circumcise the Israelites a second time." So Joshua made flint knives, and circumcised the Israelites at Gibeath-haaraloth. This is the reason why Joshua circumcised them: all the males of the people who came out of Egypt, all the warriors, had died during the journey through the wilderness after they had come out of Egypt. Although all the people who came out had been circumcised, yet all the people born on the journey through the wilderness after they had come out of Egypt had not been circumcised. (Josh 5:2–5 NRSV)

Exodus 4:1–26 complicates the puzzle even more. Zipporah circumcised her son to save his and Moses's lives. As I have noted elsewhere, "Moses avoids circumcision, indicating his lack of total conversion to the task, hinting at similar situations throughout the rest of his life. Joshua circumcised Israel in the promised land because they had not been circumcised in the wilderness (cf. Josh 5:3–5)."[1] These passages create a tension between the command in the law and the character of Moses. Moses's reputation suffers considerably when we consider the forty years in the wilderness. Moses, though Israel's leader, failed to enforce one of the cardinal rules of the covenant, which God commanded Joshua to correct. Interestingly, scholarship, which prolifically writes on circumcision and Israel's regard for the practice, has failed to consider in detail what Moses's failure here says about this great hero of ancient and modern Israel, Christianity, and Islam.

This was the context of my question in 2021 in a course on the Torah. In a lecture introducing Moses as the key figure of the Torah, I stated, "Moses must not have liked circumcision. He obviously did not enforce it during the exodus and had not circumcised his own son." This statement piqued the interest of Joshua Houston, a student in the course. I often tell students, "Good research begets more research." Similarly, scholarly musings and offhand

---

1. Bailey, *Exodus*, 97.

FOREWORD

remarks in similar contexts often launch new and very rewarding investigations and findings. After all, "Iron sharpens iron, and one person sharpens the wits of another" (Prov 27:17 NRSV).

That is the case here. Dr. Houston took the question and developed it in more detail. First, he evaluates the influence of Egyptian culture during Israel's time in Egypt both from a secular and from a religious perspective. Second, he evaluates the influence of Egyptian culture on Moses as one who lived as an Egyptian during his formative years. Third, he evaluates Joshua's circumcision of Israel's males because "although all the people who came out had been circumcised, yet all the people born on the journey through the wilderness after they had come out of Egypt had not been circumcised" (Josh 5:5 NRSV). Dr. Houston integrates the research on these three issues to emphasize the impact a dominant culture can have on another culture and its leadership. Finally, Dr. Houston's research highlights many other issues regarding circumcision in the ancient Near East that many scholars have overlooked. Any budding or mature scholar will benefit from this study because it moves them outside the biblical context and shows how the surrounding cultures influenced biblical practices (sometimes positively and sometimes negatively) while at the same time painting a clearer portrait of Moses—"Never since has there arisen a prophet in Israel like Moses, whom the LORD knew face to face" (Deut 34:10 NRSV)—but who failed to circumcise his own son and did not enforce God's command while in the wilderness.

Randall C. Bailey, PhD
Professor of Bible, VP Black College of Biblical Studies
Director, Kearley Graduate School of Theology
Faulkner University

# Preface

THIS BOOK IS A study of cultural identity, theological transformation, and historical context, focusing on the role of circumcision in the metamorphosis of the Hebrew people into national Israel. While circumcision is often viewed as a religious rite with theological significance, its role in the exodus narrative reveals deeper connections to identity, covenant, and the removal of mores brought forth by unsanctioned assimilation. By examining circumcision within the context of Egypt and the journey to Canaan, this study addresses how Israel's liberation was as much about cultural redefinition as it was about freedom from tyranny.

The genesis of this project began during my doctoral studies in a course on the Pentateuch. In a class discussion, Dr. Randall Bailey posed an intriguing observation: Moses, despite his leadership and foundational role in Israelite religion, seemed to neglect circumcision both for himself and for the Israelites during their journey in the wilderness. This observation raised my own series of questions: Why would Moses have a diminished view of circumcision? To what extent were the Israelites influenced by Egyptian cultural practices? How did those influences shape their identity during the exodus? These questions gave rise to my dissertation and ultimately to this book.

This book is written with the undergraduate and graduate student of the Hebrew Bible in mind. I realize that readers from all religious, educational, cultural, and political backgrounds are likely to pick up this book. To that end, I aim to make complex topics accessible while encouraging critical engagement with the

# Preface

biblical text and the historical material available. It is my goal to invite readers to go beyond a surface-level reading of familiar stories by considering the cultural, theological, and literary dimensions presented within the biblical narrative. This study demonstrates how ancient practices were not merely religious rituals but also tools for constructing identity and community.

The approach of this book is both historical and literary. It is my hope that this study will provide a deeper appreciation for the complexities of the biblical text. For those embarking on this study, whether as students of faith, history, or literature, I encourage you to read with both curiosity and inquisitiveness. The stories of the wilderness wanderings and Israel's journey to nationhood are far more than ancient history—they are a window into the ways in which identity, culture, and faith intersect.

# Acknowledgements

THIS WORK WOULD NOT have been possible without the guidance of the Kearley Graduate School of Theology and the financial support of the Salem Creek Church of Christ. I am especially indebted to my dissertation committee: Dr. Randall Bailey, chair, Dr. Dewayne Bryant, and Dr. G. Scott Gleaves. I am further indebted to the elders of the Salem Creek Church of Christ both present (Keith Short, Andy Melton, Andy Mitchell, Randall Phifer, B. K. Ham, Hollis Casey) and past (Jon Holland, Jim Hatfield). These men were patient with me as I labored for the congregation and labored in my intellectual pursuits. I am also grateful to the members of the Salem Creek Church of Christ's Preacher's Scholarship Committee whose financial aid I received from my time as an undergraduate student until the completion of my PhD.

No one has been more important to me in the pursuit of this project than the members of my family. I would like to thank my parents whose love and guidance are with me in whatever I pursue. Thanks also to my brother, my in-laws, and my extended family in their understanding that work on this project at times overtook our time together.

Most importantly, I want to thank my loving and supportive wife, Kayla, who provides unending inspiration and motivation. Without her support, this project would not have come to fruition.

# Abbreviations

| | |
|---|---|
| *AJT* | *American Journal of Theology* |
| *ANE* | ancient Near East |
| *ANET* | *Ancient Near Eastern Texts Relating to the Old Testament* |
| *ASR* | *American Sociological Review* |
| *BBR* | *Bulletin for Biblical Research* |
| *BibInt* | *Biblical Interpretation* |
| *BN* | *Biblishe Notizen* |
| *BRev* | *Bible Review* |
| *BSac* | *Bibliotheca Sacra* |
| *BT* | *The Bible Translator* |
| *CBQ* | *Catholic Biblical Quarterly* |
| *HAR* | *Hebrew Annual Review* |
| HB | Hebrew Bible |
| *HBT* | *Horizons in Biblical Theology* |
| *Herit* | *Sci Heritage Science* |
| *HR* | *History of Religions* |
| *HTR* | *Harvard Theological Review* |
| *JAOS* | *Journal of the American Oriental Society* |
| *JBL* | *Journal of Biblical Literature* |
| *JBQ* | *Jewish Bible Quarterly* |

## Abbreviations

| | |
|---|---|
| JBR | *Journal of Bible and Religion* |
| JEA | *Journal of Egyptian Archaeology* |
| JESHO | *Journal of the Economic and Social History of the Orient* |
| JESOT | *Journal for the Evangelical Study of the Old Testament* |
| JETS | *Journal of the Evangelical Theological Society* |
| JHE | *The Journal of Higher Education* |
| JJS | *Journal of Jesuit Studies* |
| JNSL | *Journal of Northwest Semitic Languages* |
| JQR | *Jewish Quarterly Review* |
| JSJ | *Journal for the Study of Judaism in the Persian, Hellenistic, and Roman Periods* |
| JSOT | *Journal for the Study of the Old Testament* |
| JSOTSS | *Journal for the Study of the Old Testament Supplement Series* |
| MERIP | Middle East Research and Information Project |
| *Nashim* | *Nashim: A Journal of Jewish Women's Studies & Gender Issues* |
| NT | New Testament |
| OT | Old Testament |
| PTR | *Princeton Theological Review* |
| TDNT | Theological Dictionary of the New Testament |
| *ThTo* | *Theology Today* |
| *Trad* | *Tradition: A Journal of Orthodox Jewish Thought* |
| TWOT | Theological Wordbook of the Old Testament |
| UF | *Ugarit-Forschungen* |
| *Veget Hist Archaeobot* | *Vegetation History and Archaeobotany* |

## Abbreviations

| | |
|---|---|
| VT | *Vestus Testumentum* |
| WTJ | *Westminster Theological Journal* |
| WW | *Word and World* |
| Yale JL&H | *Yale Journal of Law and the Humanities* |
| ZAW | *Zeitschrift für die Alttestamentliche Wissenschaft* |

# 1

# Introduction to the Issues

CIRCUMCISION IS NOT TYPICALLY a topic of polite conversation. You can imagine the shock when I presented this study in a church setting prior to the defense of my dissertation. I was surprised when the same level of shock occurred at a university where I was invited to give a research talk on—you guessed it—my current research. After I spoke, the dean apologized to the women in the room for my use of medical and physiological language. I am not a medical doctor, but how else can a student of Scripture study the significance of the covenant without addressing the significance of its sign (Gen 17:10)?

Circumcision fades from biblical view though remaining in its historical background after the institution and adoption of the law of Moses. Circumcision appears only once in the law of Moses (Lev 12:3) with no commentary concerning the motive behind the procedure. One may infer that the law of Moses assumes its readers already know of the Abrahamic tradition. Additionally, Sabbath observance in the law of Moses overshadows circumcision as the cult-act that is solely unique to the Hebrew people.

Outside the Hexateuch, circumcision only appears in the Hebrew Bible (hereafter, HB) as a metaphor for spiritual purity (i.e., Jer 4:4; 9:24). However, the events of the Babylonian exile (586–38 BCE) brought physical circumcision to the forefront of

# Shedding Egypt, Becoming Israel

Jewish ethnicity. Because the Israelites had no temple or land to define their identity, the Israelites placed heavier emphasis on identifying rites they could employ without a temple or land. As Farisani notes, "Under the circumstances in which the exiles lived, circumcision could thus retain its value as a sign of the covenant."[1] However, others disagree, asserting that any suggestion of circumcision's so-called "rise in significance" during the exilic period cannot be concretely known.[2] In any case, what can be known is that physical circumcision does not seem to be an issue in the HB outside of the Hexateuch.

During the Second Temple period, circumcision broadened its role as a means by which gentiles could adopt Jewish religion and identify with the Jewish people. Josephus notes that one could not become a Jew unless one had undergone circumcision (*Ant.* 20.38). Though this seems to be the consensus for most Jews of this period, for others, the gentile simply needed to reject the gods of his culture and confess Yahweh as his only God.[3] The act of circumcision undoubtedly served as the ultimate identifying mark signifying full conversion from paganism to Judaism.[4]

How did the Israelites become Israel? This question plagues scholars of both secular and religious perspectives. I will address this question more straightforwardly in chapter 5. For most scholars, Israel becomes a nation when they possess formal political leadership during the period of the judges or more radically to the period of the united monarchy. However, the identification of national Israel cannot revolve around politics since Yahweh intended to be their king (cf. Exod 6:7–8). Politics do not define a people group. The political climate in Western countries, namely the United States and Canada, make this obvious. Thus, it is to the

---

1. Farisani, "Sociological Analysis," 386.

2. Ackroyd, *Exile and Restoration*, 36.

3. Note the confessions of a certain Alexander (*Ant.* 11.331–36), Heliodorus (2 Macc 3), and Ptolemy (*Let. Aris.*). Admittedly, these examples do not reach the status of "full conversion" but demonstrate the significance of gentilic faith statements.

4. Donaldson, *Judaism and the Gentiles*, 483–92.

## Introduction to the Issues

exodus with its adventures, conflicts, and quandaries to which we must turn for the answer.

The first goal of this book is to evaluate the view of circumcision among the Israelites during the exodus considering the influence of Egyptian cultural and religious mores, Moses's view of circumcision, and Joshua's re-circumcision of the sons of Israel as the final stage of becoming national Israel. The degree to which Egypt impacted Israel in their daily life and religious practices can be evaluated by external and internal evidence. Scholars in the fields of language studies and archaeology have made great strides in linking the Israelites with a former Egyptian setting. Similarities such as the Israelite ark of the covenant and the Egyptian ark of Anubis, Yahweh's tabernacle and Egyptian military tents, Egyptian loanwords in Hebrew, and Egyptian names denote parallels between the exodus event and Egyptian culture. Scholars are also learning more about circumcision practices in ancient Egypt, which differs from ancient historical records such as those provided by Herodotus.

The second goal of this book is to evaluate Moses's view of circumcision from a narrative-critical reading of the exodus event and Moses's early life in Egypt. Because Moses lived as an Egyptian prince, his Hebraic identity, though somehow known to him (Exod 2:11), was not his primary cultural identifier. Since Moses spent his early life as an Egyptian, this study explores the possibility that Moses underwent Egyptian circumcision as an adult, thus swaying his views on the practice.

The final goal of this book is to evaluate Joshua's re-circumcision of the sons of Israel before engaging in the conquest of Canaan as the final stage in the formation of "national Israel." When the Israelites leave Egypt, they are not a nation—at least not formally. Instead, they are slaves who had been part of another culture for over four hundred years. As the exodus narrative progresses, the Egyptian cultural milieu that surrounded the Israelites sheds with the law of Moses and the giving of the promised land. Thus, the circumcision of the second generation before entering the promised land is a renewal of the Sinai covenant and the abandonment of a former Egyptianized religious rite.

# Shedding Egypt, Becoming Israel

## LIMITATIONS

Much work has been done in recent years to evaluate the impact of other cultures on Israel. Thus, limitations have been placed around the present study to narrow the scope. This study is limited to circumcision as it appears in the Hexateuch (i.e., Genesis–Joshua). It does not seek to analyze circumcision as a metaphor for spiritual purity during the prophetic age, the issue of reversing circumcision during the Hellenistic age, or baptism as the circumcision of the heart in the church age. Additionally, the study is limited to circumcision as a covenant sign and not as an identifying mark in terms of ethnicity. The process of developing an Israelite ethnic identity appears in passing in this study but does not serve as a significant part of the analysis.

Scholars have spilt much ink on the issue of Israel in Canaan and the relationship between Israel and its pagan neighbors; however, the present study is limited to an evaluation of Egyptian mores and not those of other ancient Near Eastern (hereafter ANE) cultures. Thus, an exploration of various laws in the Pentateuch and practices of the Israelites will occur retrospectively on the 430 years that Israel spent in Egypt.

Female circumcision was practiced in some cultures of the ANE as part of ritualistic or social customs, although detailed documentation is scant. It may have been linked to rites of passage, notions of purity, or preparation for marriage, reflecting the patriarchal structures of these societies. Evidence—largely derived from secondary Greek and Roman accounts—suggests its occurrence, but the specifics of its origins and its prevalence in various cultures remain a subject of scholarly debate. Because female circumcision is not an issue during the exodus event, this study is limited to circumcision as an ANE surgical procedure performed only to males. Female circumcision and debates concerning modern circumcision practices are beyond the scope of this study.

Introduction to the Issues

## DEFINITIONS OF TERMS

Because this study employs terms that are used frequently but in various ways, it is necessary to define these terms as they appear throughout the book.

"Circumcision" broadly refers to a surgical procedure that allows for the exposure of the glans and corona of the penis by making an incision in or by the full removal of the foreskin. Circumcision then refers to the procedure alone. It does not in itself denote ethnicity, religion, or the surgical degree of the procedure. However, when modified by the term "Abrahamic" (i.e., "Abrahamic circumcision"), the phrase refers to the method of circumcision that serves as a covenantal sign of Yahweh's promise to Abraham for descendants by the removal of the entire foreskin from the penis on a male child's eighth day of life according to the standard set in Gen 17 and Lev 12:3. On the other hand, "Egyptian circumcision" refers to the practice of circumcision performed in Egypt during the late Bronze Age. Archaeological evidence strongly suggests that Egyptian circumcision did not remove the entire foreskin from the penis. Instead, only a small dorsal incision was made to expose the corona and the glans. The foreskin is altered but not removed. Men entering the priesthood and royal adolescents were the most common recipients of Egyptian circumcision in the late Bronze Age.

"Social mores" (pronounced mōrēs) refer to social norms that a society observes as normative. For example, in the United States, it is the social norm to drive on the right side of the road; however, in England, the social norm is to drive on the left side. Neither is "correct" per se. Some eastern cultures use chopsticks to eat while Western cultures use forks. Again, neither option is better or worse than the other. Both reflect a cultural nuance that is understood by all who either know or are immersed in the culture.

Israel is not a nation when the people leave Egypt. I argue here that Israel does not become a nation until it possesses land and law. Thus, the phrase "Israelite metamorphosis" refers to the process by which the Hebrew people became nationalistic Israel by means of the exodus narrative. This process involved receiving the law of Moses, abandoning Egyptian cultural and religious assimilation, and receiving the promised land.

The structure of a narrative typically involves the elements of plot, setting, conflict, conflict resolution, and characters. "Characterization" refers to the literary features that describe someone or something whether obvious or hidden by the text. To notice the stylistic nuances of characterizations, this study incorporates the term "now-action" which refers to those events, decisions, movements, and thoughts demonstrated by the character within the present sequence of the narrative. I will develop the notion of now-actions further in chapter 4.

## ASSUMPTIONS

Presuppositions influence both the interpretation of texts and the methodologies employed. These assumptions—whether theological, cultural, philosophical, or historical—shape how we approach Scripture. Recognizing these presuppositions allows for a more nuanced dialogue between differing interpretive frameworks and minimizes the risk of unexamined biases dictating conclusions. To that end, I recognize that this study stands on various assumptions that are the result of years of study and intellectual contemplation. While not all will agree with the assumptions that serve as the foundation of this study, I find it necessary to share some of these assumptions before formally entering the study.

First, I assume that the biblical literature provides an adequate amount of narrative and historical allusions related to the neglect of circumcision during the exodus. I also assume that an exploration of the text within its historical and literary boundaries provides insight for Joshua's re-circumcision of second-generation Israelite men. To that end, I have diligently striven to be fair to both the historical world that lies behind the text and to the literary structure of the text. For example, when Exod 2:19 uses the description of "an Egyptian man" for Moses, the setting of Egypt (historical) and Moses's flight to Midian (narrative) are necessary to frame the scene. The actions of Ruel's daughters, while offered in thanks for Moses's intercession, may have reflected a desire to appease who they perceived as the Egyptian.

While circumcision was common in the ANE, the biblical literature provides accurate information regarding the standard for circumcision in Israel based on the narratives concerning its institution (Gen 17:9–14, 22–27) and other appearances in the Pentateuch (e.g., Gen 34:1–31; Lev 12:3). On the other hand, extrabiblical material provides information helpful to understanding circumcision in non-Israelite contexts. Though literary information regarding non-Israelite circumcision is sparse, bas-reliefs, mummies, and other archaeological features offer insight into how these practices differ from Israel's tradition.

## THE DATA AND TREATMENT OF THE DATA

This study employs two main sources of data. The primary source is the Masoretic Text (MT), the Septuagint (LXX), and English versions (New English Translation, hereafter NET, or author's translation unless otherwise noted) of the Hebrew Bible (HB). Secondary sources contain theological, historical, and literary information. Second Temple literature and archaeological findings serve to frame and emphasize the primary texts. The works of ANE sociologists and anthropologists who specialize in ancient mores and religious rites provide essential research for this study. The works of archaeologists specializing in Egyptian and Israelite history during the mid to late Bronze Age (3300–1200 BCE) provide information regarding the practice and reach of circumcision in the ANE. The works of biblical scholars who have extensively studied the Hexateuch offer insightful views of the history, purpose, and theological significance of circumcision in Israelite religion.

This study admits data from the biblical text if they relate to the formation of Israel, circumcision during the exodus event, or to the interpretation of the books of the Hexateuch. This study admits scholarly interpretation if the information establishes the current state of scholarship on the topic, demonstrates the development of the current state of scholarship, and aids in understanding circumcision in the ANE or Israel's practice of circumcision.

The methodology of this study involves the combination of historical-cultural and narrative-critical readings of the exodus narrative from the perspective of circumcision as a culturally significant religious rite and its absence as a reflection of literary characterization. This hermeneutical approach has been called a "postmodernist reading" by Aichele, Miscall, and Walsh since it blends several critical methods into one interpretive lens. In their 2009 article on postmodern biblical interpretation, they argue that the blending of various interpretive methods paves new paths for biblical studies:

> Postmodernism is characterized by diversity in both method and content and by an anti-essentialist emphasis that rejects the idea that there is a final account, an assured and agreed-on interpretation, of some one thing—here the biblical text or any part of it. Diversity in postmodernism includes not just different methods of reading and interpreting the Bible but also variety within any one method; narrative criticism, for example, is not a clear, defined approach that all narrative critics employ in the same fashion.[5]

To be sure, the Bible is literarily dependent on itself and on extrabiblical texts from the ANE. Thus, William Hallo developed the "contextual method" in which he explores how the context of the ANE shapes the text of the OT. My approach in this study mirrors Hallo's to a great degree; however, the present method gives equal weight to a narrative-critical approach in conjunction with the historical-critical reading. Since the term "postmodern" carries numerous connotations (not all of which are positive), I have adopted and adapted Hallo's "contextual" method.[6] This methodology questions the traditional characterization of Moses as "Israelite par excellence" in Second Temple Jewish theology and the perspective

---

5. Aichele et al., "Elephant in the Room," 384.

6. For a fuller discussion of Hallo's method, see Hallo, "Concept of Canonicity," 1–19.

## Introduction to the Issues

that Israelite circumcision was uninfluenced by Egyptian religious mores. This study employs a comparative analysis of ancient Near Eastern practices of circumcision and how these practices would have impacted cult rituals in Israel.

As mentioned previously, the overarching problem that this study seeks to address is the meaning of Josh 5:2, where Joshua must "circumcise again" (*wĕšŭb*) the sons of Israel "a second time" (*šēnît*). This problem rests on three subproblems. The first subproblem is to evaluate the influence of Egypt on Israelite cultural and religious mores. The data required for this analysis are in recent works on Egyptian life during the mid to late Bronze Age and works related to ancient cultural assimilation. This study analyzes Egyptian cultural and religious practices as normative, demonstrating that the Hebrew Scriptures show ties to Egyptian life and religion during the exodus.

The second subproblem is to evaluate Moses's view of circumcision in the historical context of Egypt and the literary context of the exodus narrative. This subproblem requires a narrative-critical evaluation of the exodus event and Moses's early life in Egypt. The data employed for this study are found in the book of Exodus, Philo and Josephus, the NT, and Gregory of Nyssa specifically, and other sources that deal with a narrative-critical reading of the life of Moses. A close examination of the biblical material requires an evaluation of Hebrew (MT) and Greek (LXX) grammar, syntax, and structure, namely in Exod 1–2 and Josh 5:2–9. The secondary sources served to develop a correct reading of the text where meaning or literary nuance is not obvious.

The third subproblem is to evaluate Joshua's re-circumcision of the sons of Israel before engaging in the conquest of Canaan. This subproblem requires an evaluation of the neglect of circumcision during the exodus. The data for this subproblem are found in Hebrew and Greek texts of Exodus and Joshua and in recent works of ANE historians who specialize in cult rites and national identity. This analysis requires a grammatical, syntactical, and contextual study of Josh 5:2–9 and an evaluation of Israel's metamorphosis in the Hexateuch. More specifically, the terms *wĕšŭb* and *šēnît* in

Josh 5:2 deserve special attention alongside a syntactical study of the Josh 5:2–9 pericope in the LXX.

## A BRIEF REVIEW OF THE CURRENT LITERATURE

While space does not allow for a discussion of every work on Egypt, the exodus, Moses, and circumcision, the works mentioned below are those that this study found most insightful given their connection to the issues of the various subproblems. The study employs and interacts with far more literature than the few mentioned below; however, a short discussion of the present fields of Egyptology and Pentateuchal studies proves beneficial.

The first subproblem questions the influence of Egypt on Israelite cultural and religious mores. The related hypothesis suggests that the influence of Egypt on Israelite mores reveals the Israelites practiced an Egyptian form of circumcision in place of Abrahamic circumcision. One cannot engage in a study of the cultural context of the ANE without encountering Kenneth Kitchen's seminal work *On the Reliability of the Old Testament*. Kitchen paints with a broad brush as he introduces a vast amount of evidence for the historical reliability of the HB. Kitchen convincingly shows that—whether one thinks of the exodus as a historical event or only a theme within ancient Hebraic thought—the exodus is the most significant event in the HB. While Kitchen also provides an analysis of the conquest, he does not expound on circumcision either in the ANE or in Israelite religion, nor does he comment on the gap in circumcision practices as inferred by Josh 5:2–9. Kitchen's purpose is much broader. He seeks to answer if the books of the HB provide accurate historical information. The exodus and conquest serve only as a small, but significant, part of Kitchen's overall study.

John Currid's book *Ancient Egypt* fills in the gaps concerning Egypt's relationship to the Hebrews, from creation myths to prophecy. Currid addresses Egyptian symbolism in the Pentateuch and the Egyptian background of the plagues, the serpent confrontation of Moses and the Egyptian magicians, and the bronze serpent pericope; however, he does not connect Israelite behavior to cultural

## Introduction to the Issues

assimilation.[7] Jack Sasson's work narrowly fills this gap, namely by analyzing circumcision in the ANE. This places the problem of Josh 5:2–9 against its historical backdrop. Sasson observes, "Whereas the Hebrews amputated the prepuce and thus exposed the corona of the penis, the Egyptian practice consisted of a dorsal incision upon the foreskin which liberated the glans penis."[8] Sasson demonstrates how Egyptian mores impacted Israelite religious customs; however, Sasson does not address whether circumcision was voluntary for Egyptians (as it was not for Israelite boys) or whether the Hebrews of the exodus only circumcised their priests and officials as was the practice of the Egyptians.

James Boice does not view Joshua's re-circumcision narrative negatively. Instead, Boice views the narrative as ironic given Israel's recovery from the surgery provided a prime opportunity for enemy attack. Boice suggests that Yahweh spares Israel from annihilation at its most vulnerable state, echoing the events of Gen 34.[9] Boice's observation is not without merit; however, Boice ignores Josh 5:9, which describes the circumcision as the removal of the "disgrace of Egypt."

Egyptologists agree that "even though male circumcision was practiced in Egypt from predynastic times, very little direct evidence about the operation itself is available from the millennia of Egyptian history."[10] Fortunately, James Hoffmeier's work acknowledges these assimilations. Hoffmeier, though an evangelical scholar, is not an apologist for the text. Assuming a late date for the exodus, Hoffmeier argues Israel maintained aspects of Egyptian religion in its tabernacle and later temple cult practices. Hoffmeier is less concerned with whether the exodus happened than he is with what history proves concerning the exodus. Hoffmeier leaves room for further study in that he does not address the exodus as theologically connected to Egyptian religion. Not all scholars are

7. Currid, *Ancient Egypt*, 1997.
8. Sasson, "Circumcision," 474.
9. Boice, *Joshua*, 41.
10. Megahed and Vymazalová, "Ancient Egyptian Royal Circumcision," 158.

convinced of Egyptian influence on Israel. These scholars view Moses as a created hero for Israel and the exodus as a grandiose account of Israel's formation. Dever suggests, "It would be easy to conclude, along with Freud's classic study *Moses and Monotheism*, that Moses was simply invented out of deep subconscious human desires." For Dever (and others in his camp), Moses and the law are "simply part of second-century-BC origin myths and have no historical basis." This view is paramount among critical scholars of the Pentateuch and the exodus. Dever's work *Who Were the Early Israelites and Where Did They Come From?* provides necessary dialogue with Hoffmeier.[11]

The second subproblem narrows the scope to evaluate Moses's view of circumcision in his historical context of Egypt and the literary context of the exodus narrative. The related hypothesis suggests that an evaluation of Moses's view of circumcision in an Egyptian historical context will reveal Moses's upbringing as an Egyptian influenced his view of circumcision. Ancient Jewish historians comment on Moses's life in Egypt and Midian.[12] Philo and Josephus demonstrate Jewish thought regarding Moses in the late Second Temple period. For Philo, Moses is the ideal Platonic philosopher-king (*Mos.* 1.5.23). Josephus's work *Antiquity of the Jews* expounds on the Jewish tradition regarding Moses's life in Egypt (*Ant.* 2.10.1–2).

J. P. Peters suggests, "[Moses] grew up under the protection of the Egyptian princess, but himself conscious of his Israelite origin."[13] Moses obviously knew the Hebrew people were his people (cf. Exod 2:11; *wayēṣēʾ ʾel-ʾeḥāyw*), but how familiar Moses was with his people's religious customs while living as an Egyptian cannot be known. These religious customs are also speculative since the law did not yet exist. At best, one may assume the Israelites

---

11. See Dever, *Who Were the Early Israelites?*, 235.

12. Acts 7:20–42 and Heb 11:24–28 demonstrate interpretations of Moses within the first-century Jewish community. However, both interpretations do not match the character of Moses of the exodus who shuns circumcision and abandons his people.

13. Peters, "Religion of Moses," 105.

## Introduction to the Issues

practiced sacrifice and circumcision based on the prominence of these practices in Genesis. However, these assumptions are merely that. There is no way to know what the worship of Yahweh (if any at all) looked like during the Egyptian captivity.

Sigmund Freud accepted Moses as strictly Egyptian, which places Moses as a gentile and thereby would hold little authority in Israelite culture. This contradicts Philo's view of Moses as a devout Israelite even in Midian (cf. Philo, *De Vita Mosis* 1.47). These observations allow the present study to blend Moses's multiethnicity into one literary character impacted by his historical-cultural molding.

Critical scholarship has long focused on "Moses the Israelite" rather than "Moses the Egyptian" or "Moses the Midianite." Understanding Moses's upbringing in Egypt and midlife in Midian are vital to understanding his personal development. An exploration of the impact of Moses's birth parents, Pharaoh's daughter, and Moses's father-in-law as cultural and religious influences is necessary. Thomas Dozeman suggests that Pharaoh's daughter's identification of Moses as a Hebrew in Exod 2:6 is a literary device intended to separate the Hebrews from the Egyptians.[14] Dozeman adds, "The birth story of Moses is not intended to make Moses Egyptian but to place him in Egyptian culture."[15] However, Hoffmeier suggests all Israelites underwent a baptism of Egyptian culture.[16] Given the evidence from the biblical narrative, Hoffmeier is more convincing. The lack of consensus concerning Moses's pre-exodus identity demands an evaluation of his cultural assimilation.

Moses's Midianite context has received little scholarly attention. Martin Noth observes the Midian narrative as it relates to the flight narrative and call narrative; however, Noth neglects any real observation of Midianite customs that might result in the

---

14. Dozeman, *Exodus*, 84.

15. Dozeman, *Exodus*, 84.

16. Hoffmeier has proven this point in his work *Ancient Israel in Sinai*. All Israelites assimilated in some form to Egyptian culture, and Moses even more. Stephen says in Acts 7:22 that Moses "was instructed in all the ways of the Egyptians." While Israelite slaves may not have been able to read or write, Moses undoubtedly could as a royal Egyptian.

## Shedding Egypt, Becoming Israel

literary characterization of Moses.[17] George Coats suggests understanding Midianite marriage customs is key to understanding the bridegroom of blood pericope in Exod 4:24–26.[18] Coats connects the marriage custom of Midian to circumcision, which suggests Moses's son had not yet been married and thus had not received circumcision as a Midianite prenuptial rite.[19] If this is true, Moses had adopted the cultural mores of his father-in-law.

The third subproblem is to evaluate Joshua's re-circumcision of the sons of Israel before engaging in the conquest of Canaan. The related hypothesis suggests that Joshua's re-circumcision of the sons of Israel serves as the final stage in Israel's national metamorphosis. To that end, the exodus event must serve as an unfolding narrative. Few scholars have noted the issue of the circumcision narrative of Josh 5:2–9 as denoting some kind of malpractice during the wilderness wanderings.[20] This literature review introduces foundational works on the institution, purpose, and function of circumcision in Israel from Abraham to Joshua.

Matthew Thiessen is among the most recent scholars to evaluate the socioreligious function of circumcision in Israel. Thiessen received his PhD in New Testament from Duke University and has become a foremost scholar on gentile inclusion in Jewish religion and the ethnic identity of the Jews. Thiessen's book *Contesting Conversion: Genealogy, Circumcision, and Identity in Ancient Judaism and Christianity* delves into the complex nature of religious conversion within the Israelite context, exploring the historical, cultural, and religious dimensions of circumcision as a central element of Jewish identity. Most scholars rely on the Priestly (P) source, suggesting circumcision arises during the exile as a religious and ethnic identifier.[21] Thiessen concludes, "Eighth-day circumcision functioned to weave together Jewish practices

---

17. See Noth, *Exodus*.
18. Coats, "Moses in Midian," 9.
19. Coats, "Moses in Midian," 9.
20. For example, Krause, "Das Buch Josua Auf Griechisch," 23–58; Farber, *Images of Joshua*.
21. Thiessen, *Contesting Conversion*, 7.

## Introduction to the Issues

with proper genealogical descent."[22] However, Thiessen's analysis is incomplete since he avoids any discussion of valid non-eighth-day circumcisions like the circumcision of Abraham, Ishmael, and the men in Abraham's house and the re-circumcision narrative of Josh 5:2–9.[23]

Shaye Cohen performs a meticulous examination of the historical origins and development of Jewish identity in terms of "otherness." Cohen's book *The Beginnings of Jewishness: Boundaries, Varieties, and Uncertainties* explores ancient Jewish texts and traditions, offering an analysis of the significance of circumcision within the early Jewish community.[24] By exploring the cultural, religious, and social contexts surrounding circumcision, Cohen traces the evolution of circumcision as the central ritual for the formation of Jewish identity. He explores symbolic meanings of circumcision and its role in establishing and maintaining boundaries of Jewishness. His observations concerning circumcision as community identity places the Israelites in an "us/them" dichotomy, which dangerously ignores possible ANE influences on Israelite culture. His observations call for a broadening evaluation of circumcision, placing the act in ANE contexts rather than in an Israelite context alone.

Studies of circumcision in Israel stand on the shoulders of Andreas Blaschke's work *Beschneidung: Zeugnisse der Bibel und verwandter Texte*.[25] By analyzing relevant biblical passages and exploring their linguistic, literary, and theological dimensions, Blaschke sheds light on the symbolic, ritualistic, and communal significance of circumcision in ancient Israel. The work offers an account of the history and importance of Israelite circumcision from its beginnings to the first decades of the second century AD. The study takes the form of a comprehensively annotated collection of sources including Israelite, pagan, and Christian texts.

---

22. Thiessen, *Contesting Conversion*, 143.
23. Also Exod 4:25 and Gen 34.
24. Cohen, *Beginnings of Jewishness*, 2, 11–12.
25. Blaschke, *Beschneidung*.

While Blaschke's work serves as a reference on circumcision, the book lacks any analysis of Joshua's circumcision of second-generation men, which the present study seeks to fill.

David Bernat's book *Sign of the Covenant: Circumcision in the Priestly Tradition* explores the religious, legal, and ethical aspects of circumcision. Bernat examines the significance of circumcision within the context of Jewish law, providing a comprehensive analysis of its theological foundations and its role as a central ritual in Israelite identity. Bernat explores the nature of the covenant and the principles of bodily integrity. He also engages with contemporary debates related to circumcision in Israel. For Bernat, Israelite circumcision places Israel in its own camp. However, Bernat ignores circumcision as a pre-Israelite practice (i.e., before Jacob and his sons) and narrative readings outside the P source. While Bernat's work is significant in recognizing circumcision as an identifying rite, the present study fills Bernat's gap by exploring circumcision as formative and not merely a Hebraic afterthought for identity in Babylonian exile.

Karl Deenick's book *Righteous by Promise: A Biblical Theology of Circumcision* helpfully bridges the gap between ritual and theology. Deenick traces the themes of circumcision, seed, faith, and righteousness throughout the HB and the NT, developing a framework in which circumcision represents obedience and faith. Deenick concludes, "Circumcision is unavoidably bound up with both the demand and promise of righteousness/blamelessness."[26] This presents a contrast to Thiessen and Cohen who view circumcision as an identifying mark with little theological repercussions. However, Deenick does not give attention to the hermeneutical shifts of circumcision from its institution to the Babylonian exile. For example, circumcision begins as a sign of the covenant that looks ahead, though the act soon transitions to a sign of a people group, then to a metaphor for spiritual purity in the prophets. Joshua's circumcision of Israelite men denotes a hermeneutical

---

26. Deenick, *Righteous by Promise*, 211.

## Introduction to the Issues

shift in the interpretation of Abrahamic circumcision from a future promise to a present reality.

Narrative-critical evaluations of the Pentateuch abound.[27] Here, the focus will be on those observations that center on the development of national Israel.[28] Such observations are ancient and progress to the modern day.[29] One scarcely engages in a discussion of biblical narrative without encountering the works of Robert Alter. Alter's book *The Art of Biblical Narrative* explores the complexities of Hebrew narrative by analyzing plot, point of view, and characterization:

> Biblical narrative offers us, after all, nothing in the way of minute analysis or detailed rendering of mental processes; whatever indications we may be vouchsafed of feeling, attitude, or intention are rather minimal; and we are given only the barest hints about the physical appearance, the tics and gestures, the dress and implements of the characters, the material milieu in which they enact their destinies. In short, all the indicators of nuanced individuality to which the Western literary tradition has accustomed us—preeminently in the novel, but ultimately going back to the Greek epics and romances—would appear to be absent from the Bible.[30]

Alter observes that the HB is often silent concerning personal characterization. When character details appear (e.g., that Saul was tall or that Rachel was beautiful), the reader needs to take

---

27. Barton, "Law and Narrative," 126–40; Thompson and Irvin, "Joseph and Moses Narratives," 149–212; Goswell, "Non-Royal Portrayal," 60–81; Dozeman, Römer, and Schmid, *Pentateuch, Hexateuch, or Enneateuch?*; Kanarek, *Biblical Narrative*.

28. The issue of the historical Moses is beyond the scope of this project. Scholars have addressed this issue elsewhere. When this project speaks of "Moses," it denotes Moses as a literary character. See McDermott, *Reading the Pentateuch*.

29. Both Josephus and Philo paint favorable pictures of the exodus and its leaders. For a fuller analysis, see Feldman, "Josephus's Portrait of Moses," 285–328. See also Feldman, "Moses in Midian," 1–20.

30. Alter, *Art of Biblical Narrative*, 143.

special notice. Given that the biblical material says little concerning Israel's circumcision rituals during the Egyptian captivity and the exodus, the reader must fill in these gaps based on later narrative events. Biblical characterization is often unpredictable and changing.[31] Alter does not speculate concerning Moses's life in Egypt or Midian or concerning Joshua's role beyond successor to Moses. Given that Alter is only concerned with the text's portrayal of the character, he does not step beyond the text's description. The present study also does not seek to go beyond the text but will cultivate narrative elements based on cultural context where Alter does not.

Harold Bloom suggests that Moses's role as the leader of Israel meant less to the Yahwist (J) and Deuteronomistic (D) sources but is more significant in the Priestly (P) and Elohist (E) sources.[32] However, the final form of the Hexateuch serve as authoritative texts within the Jewish religious community. To that end, Brevard Childs's canonical-critical method proves useful over Wellhausen's documentary hypothesis, though this is not to discredit Wellhausen's contributions.[33] While some have argued that his methods revert to a "proto-critical method" of interpretation, this is not the case.[34] Childs's method raises the question of which interpretive lens is correct—Jewish, Protestant, Catholic, or higher-critical?[35]

31. Alter, *Art of Biblical Narrative*, 158.

32. Bloom, "From J to K," 22.

33. The discovery of a curse tablet at Mt. Ebal presents the names *el* and *Yahweh* together in a proto-Canaanite script. The discovery is so recent, one cannot say to what degree these implications will be for the documentary hypothesis. For this study, the documentary hypothesis will remain a valid option for Pentateuchal source critical studies. For more on the curse tablet, see Stripling et al., "'You Are Cursed,'" 1–24. See also Baden, *Composition of the Pentateuch*, 14; Kittel, "Brevard Childs's Development," 2.

34. Walter Brueggemann observes this phenomenon and offers extensive comments in his 1989 article "Brevard Childs's Canonical Criticism: An Example of Post-Critical Naiveté."

35. Barton argues, "If it is essentially the Christian or Jewish community that defines the limits of the Old Testament canon, does that not mean that the interpreter is under some constraint, not just to read the particular form of the Old Testament his community accepts, but also to read it in the manner

## Introduction to the Issues

James Barr criticizes Childs's use of the MT over the LXX because the church preferred the MT.[36] Yet, for narrative-critical readings, the text that better reflects the community better reflects the trend of the narrative. Childs's use of the MT reflects the Jewish community. However, as in the case of Josh 5:2–9, the LXX offers a variant reading that must be considered within a canonical perspective.

Randall Bailey's commentary on Exodus expresses the need to blend critical approaches regarding the exodus and Moses but does not formally do so. Observing the bridegroom of blood pericope, Bailey observes, "On the one level [Exod 4:24–26 and Josh 5:2–9] indicate that Moses did not like circumcision," which leads to speculation regarding the relationship between the Mosaic and Abrahamic covenants.[37] Bailey does not provide an answer as to why Moses did not like circumcision.[38] Additionally, Bailey notes that Exod 4:24–26 depicts Moses as negligent, though it is not clear whether Moses would have known about Abrahamic circumcision given his non-Hebraic early life. Bailey's observations call for a deeper narrative-critical reading of Moses alongside the Hebrews as both entities must transition from Egyptian to Israelite.

## THE IMPORTANCE OF THE STUDY

Scholars have yet to address circumcision's place among the Israelites during the exodus. Regarding circumcision broadly, Bernat observes the lack of scholarly attention:

---

his community regards as normative?" Barton, *Reading the Old Testament*, 95.

36. This preference dates to Jerome's idea of "Hebraica veritas." See Barr, "Childs's Introduction," 22.

37. Bailey, *Exodus*, 97.

38. Scholarly views on the bridegroom of blood pericope abound, yet none address why Moses neglected circumcision. Pamela Reis argues the bridegroom of blood pericope mirrors the call of Abraham. Based on rabbinic tradition, Maller believes the pericope demonstrates Moses's guilt. Gorospe employs a narrative-critical approach, suggesting the pericope demonstrates Moses's transition from Midianite to leader of the Hebrews. Hamilton connects the passage to Balaam. See Reis, "Bridegroom of Blood," 324–31; Maller, "Bridegroom of Blood," 94–98; Gorospe, *Narrative and Identity*; Hamilton. *Exodus*.

## Shedding Egypt, Becoming Israel

> Despite the importance attributed to circumcision in the Hebrew Bible, the topic has not been accorded sufficient attention in the scholarship. . . . Studies of circumcision have been more narrowly focused, on individual biblical passages or topics, while attempts at synthesis tend toward summary, appearing as entries in encyclopedias, excurses in commentaries, chapters of larger works, and brief notes in survey literature.[39]

While this study does not develop a biblical or systematic theology of circumcision (others have done this elsewhere), this study adds to the conversation of circumcision's role in Israel by evaluating it as a prerequisite for national identity.

While scholars have commented on the circumcision narrative of Josh 5:2–9 and the bridegroom of blood pericope of Exod 4:24–26 specifically, scholars have not yet asked why these odd circumcision narratives appear as a form of valid circumcision though the fullest standard of the law is not obeyed. This study approaches the exodus as the metamorphosis of the Hebrews from Bedouins to a sovereign nation. Scholars have missed the re-circumcision narrative of Josh 5:2–9 as a formative stage in Israel's national development—what this study calls "becoming Israel." Since circumcision appears as a significant rite in multiple ANE cultures during the time of the exodus, this study places circumcision in terms of citizenship and covenant renewal.

## The Organization of the Study

The first chapter has stated the problem and subproblems, defined terms, listed assumptions and hypotheses, provided an overview of relevant literature to the study, and introduced the need for the study. The second and third chapters examine the influence of Egypt on Israel from a historical-critical perspective. The fourth chapter places Moses in his Egyptian context, exploring the proposition that Moses underwent circumcision as a royal young adult and thereby developed a contempt for the practice.

---

39. Bernat, *Sign of the Covenant*, 1–2.

INTRODUCTION TO THE ISSUES

The fourth chapter places the circumcision narrative of Josh 5:2–9 in the greater context of "becoming Israelite" to which features of the exodus narrative demonstrate the shedding of Egyptian mores and the development of Israel as a nation. The fifth chapter offers a summary, conclusion, and recommendations for further research.

# 2

# The Influence of Egypt on Israel's Secular Mores

ISRAEL'S EXPERIENCE WITH EGYPT was integral to its historical-cultural setting.[1] For example, Abraham travelled to Egypt shortly after his call (Gen 12:10–20), Joseph became a slave to a high-ranking Egyptian official (Gen 39:1–6), and the early tribes of Israel moved to Egypt to escape famine (Gen 46:3–7).[2] Because of their close connections, John Currid notes, "There is no question that the Egyptians and the Hebrews borrowed many things from one another."[3] Joshua 5:8 suggests that although the Hebrews had wandered in the wilderness for forty years, the disgrace of Egypt remained on the people.[4] Commentators differ on what

---

1. Dalman, "Egypt and Early Israel's Cultural Setting," 449.

2. The travels to Egypt in Genesis form a chiasm. Shortly after Abram's call to "go out from your country, your relatives, and your household to the land that I (Yahweh) will show you," Abram goes to Egypt with his nephew, Lot, and his possessions. Abram left his homeland, but he did not leave his relatives (i.e., Lot) or his household (i.e., his possessions) and did not follow Yahweh but went to the "safe place" of Egyptian comfort.

3. Currid, *Ancient Egypt*, 26.

4. Kidner notes, "As for Egypt's impressive temples, gods, and obelisks, so reassuring to this superstitious company, all such things would prove merely combustible, portable or breakable, and the whole land as easily picked up and put on by a conqueror as a cloak by a shepherd." Kidner, *Jeremiah*, 132.

## The Influence of Egypt on Israel's Secular Mores

this "disgrace" specifically is. Though many reject the connection, the text aligns the re-circumcision of these Israelite men as one of many ways in which Yahweh removes this disgrace. We will revisit this hypothesis in chapter 5. What can be known at face value here is that some aspect of Egypt remained at the forefront of Israelite identity throughout the exodus event. Regarding Exod 2:1–10, Gordon Davies notes the Hebrews' struggle to transition from Egyptian to Israelite:

> The question, "Whom will we serve, God or Pharaoh?" can be recast in terms of historical self-understanding: "Who are the Israelites in the light of their past?" The answer that Israel will give is a choice between creation and destruction, integration, and chaos.[5]

Davies's recognition of Israel's past emphasizes the shedding of cultural mores throughout the exodus narrative. This chapter examines the influence of Egypt on Israel from a historical-critical perspective, identifying Egyptian influences on pre-conquest Israelite culture.

Scholarly views regarding Israelite assimilation tend to fall on two extremes. Scholars in the 1970s championed a method that sought to exploit the parallels of social and religious practices between surrounding ANE texts and Israelite literature.[6] John Van Seters argued that the parallel information provided enough concrete evidence to support these claims.[7] Gösta Ahlström's 1986 work *Who Were the Israelites?* intended to uncover Israel's origin without using the Pentateuch.[8] Most of the scholarly debate regarding the exodus and the formation of Israel relies on the presupposition of whether or not the exodus occurred as a historical event.[9] On

---

5. Davies, *Israel in Egypt*, 117.

6. Hoffmeier, *Israel in Egypt*, 4.

7. Van Seters employed a comparative approach extending beyond, but including, ANE documents. Van Seters explores Greek documents and Israel's own historiography. Others, such as Thompson, follow suit. See Van Seters, *In Search of History*, 7.

8. See Ahlström. *Who Were the Israelites?*.

9. Hoffmeier, *Israel in Egypt*, 4.

the other hand, more apologetic scholars view Israel in a cultural vacuum. Such scholars recognize Israel's nature of separationism.[10] However, Israel does not exist in a historical-cultural void. The HB places the exodus as Yahweh's demonstration of power, authority, and sovereignty over Egypt first and subsequently other nations. Thus, the exodus narrative provides details concerning the Israelites' relationship between Egypt and themselves.

Less explored is the literary perspective of Egypt as it exists in the minds of the literary characters compared to the mind of the narrator/author. For example, when famine strikes, Abram goes to Egypt to get food —a good thing to do in his mind. However, the narrator is quick to express the conflict caused by Abram's association with Egypt as Sarai becomes endangered (cf. Gen 12:10–20). The narrative of Hagar and Ishmael offers a parallel. Hagar is an Egyptian slave. In the mind of the characters (i.e., Abram and Sarai), using the Egyptian as a surrogate would be a good thing; however, to the mind of the narrator, the use of the Egyptian would not bring the intended result and would develop otherwise avoidable conflict (cf. Gen 16). This pattern extends throughout the HB, namely in the prophetic books (e.g., Isa 30 and Jer 42).

## MATTERS OF DAILY LIFE

The adoption of Egyptian names among the Israelites, the plundering of Egyptian clothing, and cravings for Egyptian food during the exodus suggest a high level of Egyptian acculturation. Biblical tradition places the Hebrews in Egypt for multiple generations.[11]

---

10. For example, Hendel observes, "Ancient Israel was a nation in the Near East, but it conceived of itself as a unique people." See Hendel, "Israel Among the Nations," 3.

11. Determining the chronology of this event is difficult from the biblical text and archeological evidence. Exodus 12:40 states that the Israelites dwelt in Egypt for 430 years. Genesis 15:13 predicts a period of captivity for 400 years. Rashi, having recalculated the chronology, asserted Israel was in Egypt for 210 years. The rabbis explain that the prophecy in Gen 15 took place 30 years prior to the birth of Isaac; thus, 430 in Exodus refers to the time since Gen 15. Paul argues in Gal 3:17 that the law came 430 years after Abraham's call (based on

## The Influence of Egypt on Israel's Secular Mores

Sociologists suggest that acculturation can occur as quickly as a few weeks.[12] In other words, it only takes a matter of weeks to become familiar enough with a culture to adopt some of its mores. For example, if I, a Southern American man, went to Zimbabwe, it would only take a few weeks or less to learn how to operate according to their customs, such as their dining habits or dress. Though scholars debate the exact chronology of Israel's period in Egypt, the biblical narrative presents a history of multigenerational captives (cf. Num 1:1–4). The biblical text demonstrates that the older generations passed down their learned behavior to the younger generations.

There is a gap between Hebrew and Egyptian culture to be sure, but to what degree this gap existed is difficult to say. A further complication is the language barrier or lack thereof between the Egyptians and the Semitic language of the Israelites. If Joseph's era coincided with the Hyksos period, communication may not have been a problem since they too were Semitic. The international trade of the time and documents from the Amarna period suggests that communication might not have been as great of an issue as formerly thought. When Abraham goes to Egypt in Gen 12:10–20, the text does not imply that a translator or interpreter aided in his conversation with the Pharaoh. The same is true with the Joseph narrative. However, it does not seem plausible that the high Egyptian officials (non-Hyksos) would have known these Semitic languages. It is more plausible then—given Egypt's status as the dominant world power at the time of the exodus—that other cultures knew the Egyptian language and were not ignorant concerning Egyptian cultural frameworks. Suffice it here to say whether the gap between Hebrew and Egyptian culture was broad or narrow, a gap existed nonetheless.

---

Stephen's speech in Acts 7). Adopting this approach accounts for the 400 and 430 years recorded. It is beyond the scope of this study to address specific matters of chronology. What is significant is that the narrative places the Hebrews as multigenerational captives. See Gadeloff, "How Long," 183–89.

12. Debate abounds concerning the definition and various uses of the terms "assimilation" and "acculturation" in their respective contexts. See Schachter, "From 'Different' to 'Similar,'" 981–1013.

## Names

The practice of placing Egyptian names on Hebrew children begins with Joseph:

> But the name *Manasseh* is not a Hebrew but an Egyptian word; while the name *Ephraim* is par excellence a Hebrew word. There is a strong probability then that while Ephraim meant the Hebrew division of the emigration, Manasseh meant the "mixed multitude," partly Egyptian and partly perhaps Kenite, Midianite, or what not. The word Manasseh reappears in Hebrew history, after the lapse of 500 years, as the name of a king of Judah (not of Israel); and evidently not a survival of what had been a common personal or family name, but as an Egyptian name; for, it comes to view in company with other Egyptian names, and in consequence of the alliance of Solomon with a reigning Pharaoh, whose daughter he made his queen, or first lady of the harem.[13]

Not all agree with the above conclusion. For example, some scholars accept the name "Manasseh" (*měnašeh*) as a Piel participle meaning "the one who brings about forgetfulness."[14] The commentators of the NET suggest that "the giving of this Hebrew name to his son shows that Joseph retained his heritage and faith."[15] While Lesley suggested above that Ephraim is a Hebrew name, Delitzsch suggests "Ephraim" (*'epraîm*) is a form of the Hebrew verb *pārāh* meaning "to bear fruit."[16] Spurrell and Fontinoy assert a Hebrew meaning for "fruitfulness" as an idiom for prosperity.[17] These perspectives ignore Joseph's Egyptian setting, namely that his wife, Asenath, is the daughter of Potiphera, an Egyptian priest of On who would have led the worship of Ra. Joseph's marriage to Asenath cemented his place in Egyptian society. Additionally, this would

---

13. Lesley, "Notes," 411.
14. *HALOT*, s.v. "מְנַשֶּׁה."
15. "NET Notes," n99 at Gen 41:51.
16. Delitzsch, *New Commentary on Genesis*, 305.
17. Hoffmeier does not comment on this name. See Spurrell, *Notes*, 334; Fontinoy, "Les noms," 33–40.

## The Influence of Egypt on Israel's Secular Mores

have removed doubt about Pharaoh's approval. Though evidence abounds regarding the etymology of the names "Ephraim" and "Manasseh," Joseph's life in Potiphar's home, Joseph's connection to Pharaoh, having an Egyptian priest as his father-in-law, having an Egyptian wife, and receiving Egyptian burial rites demonstrates Joseph's acceptance of and assimilation to Egyptian culture.[18]

Following Lesley's argument that the name "Manasseh" is an Egyptian name, one can confidently conclude that the trend of Egyptian assimilation began with Joseph and continued into the period of the Israelite captivity. Several scholars have noted the presence of Egyptian names among the Hebrews elsewhere; however, these analyses often serve as linguistic studies for the development of either the Hebrew or Egyptian language and not as establishing a closer cultural overlap.[19] The goal here is not to establish a historicity of Israel in Egypt or a study of linguistics. Rather, the goal is to establish a trend of Egyptian practices accepted by the Hebrews.

James Hoffmeier, expounding on the previous work of Theophile Meek, observes that there are six names which are "unquestionably Egyptian": Moses, Assir, Phineas, Hophni, Merari, and Pashhur.[20] The presence of Egyptian names occurs most notably among the generations of the Levites.[21] Though Jochebed does not

---

18. Many have asserted that Joseph was in Egypt during the reign of the Hyksos. However, scholars note that the Hyksos accepted and assimilated (to the best of their abilities) to Egyptian religion and culture. Furthermore, Genesis refers to Potiphar as "the Egyptian" (Gen 39:1). If Joseph is in Egypt, why would the author comment that Potiphar was Egyptian? Others have recognized this may allude to a time when being an Egyptian in Egypt was rare (i.e., the Hyksos invasion). So, even if Joseph was in Egypt during the Hyksos invasion, Joseph still lived in an Egyptian home for a time and served under an Egyptian-assimilated culture. Redford, "Hyksos Invasion," 7–8.

19. Lambdin, Wilson, and others have extensively studied the use of Egyptian loanwords in the OT. See Lambdin, "Egyptian Loan Words," 145–55; Wilson, "Foreign Words," 177–247; cf. Rubin, "Egyptian Loanwords," 1.793–94; Muchiki, *Egyptian Proper Names and Loanwords*.

20. These names led Meek to believe that at least some Hebrews had been in Egypt. See Hoffmeier, *Ancient Israel in Sinai*, 223.

21. Hoffmeier, *Ancient Israel in Sinai*, 230.

## Shedding Egypt, Becoming Israel

name Moses, she and Amram bestow Egyptian names on Moses's brother, Aaron, and sister, Miriam. These names do not seem to have any Semitic origins.[22] The name "Aaron" may derive from the Egyptian word for "overseer," which has priestly connotations.[23] Additionally, the name could derive from the Egyptian word for "tent," which may connect to the priestly role in the "tent of meeting."[24] Regarding the name "Miriam," Gardiner suggests the name also has an Egyptian etymology:

> If, in the teeth of all objections, the Egyptian origin of Moses be upheld, then why not also that of Miriam and of Mary, the later equivalent of Miriam? In my opinion, at least as good a case can be made out for an Egyptian derivation of Miriam as has been made for Moses.[25]

The name "Miriam" may reflect the Egyptian phrase "beloved of Amun," indicating a connection to the Egyptian deity.[26] If Miriam is an Egyptian name, each of Amram and Jochebed's children bore Egyptian names whether bestowed on them by their parents or by another party.[27] Eduard Meyer suggests that Egyptian names ran in the family of Moses.[28] To use the language of "ran in" im-

---

22. Noth, *Die Israelitischen*, 3.

23. Hoffmeier, *Ancient Israel in Sinai*, 224.

24. The Egyptian alphabet did not have a *lamed*. In cases when a *lamed* was needed, the Egyptians would use an "*r*." Homan connects the Hebrew term for "tent" (*'ōhel*) to the name "Aaron" (*'ahărōn*). The suffix would render the name as "tent-man." Demotic, which appears around 650 BCE, does include a *lamed*; however, this is a later development than what is at stake here. See Allen, *Middle Egyptian*, 16–17; Homan, "Tensile Etymology for Aaron," 21–22.

25. Gardiner, "Egyptian Origin," 194.

26. Hartmann, "Mose und Maria," 621.

27. Amram is absent in the narrative of Exod 2. Additionally, the narrative does not give the names of Amram or Jochebed. Moses is born at a time when Pharaoh commands the Hebrew midwives to kill the male children immediately following their birth (Exod 1:16). Exodus 2 gives no better evidence since the author informs the reader only of Jochebed's actions, not her character. To phrase it differently, the text does not tell the reader of Amram and Jochebed's religious piety. At most, one sees a loving mother who makes an ample effort to ensure her child's survival.

28. Meyer, *Geschichte des Altertums*, 2, 208.

plies a history of Egyptian names passed down from generation to generation. The names of Aaron and Moses do not appear in later Israelite genealogies in the HB. The name "Miriam" appears in 1 Chron 4:17; however, this name appears in the line of Judah rather than the line of Levi.[29] If Egyptian names "ran in" Moses's familial heritage, one would expect to see these names appearing in later genealogies, but this is not the case. The better observation is that Egyptian names did not "run in" Amram and Jochebed's family but that their children received their names as the result of their historical context.

The text does not record a name bestowed on Moses by his biological parents. Given that Aaron and Miriam have Egyptian names, it is plausible that Moses also had an Egyptian name prior to his naming by Pharaoh's daughter. Hartmann observes the tension between the consonantal and vowel possibilities of the Hebrew and Egyptian name "Moses":

> In the past there have been numerous ideas about the Egyptian root of the name "Moses." Vocal and consonantal differences between Egyptian and Hebrew were repeatedly taken into account. In addition, the unnecessary cultural connection between biblical names and Egyptian examples was questioned.[30]

Scholars generally agree that the name "Moses" is exclusively Egyptian and likely a shortened form of a longer name that included the name of an Egyptian deity. Harttmann suggests that over time in monotheistic Israel, the theophoric element of Moses's name likely dropped out.[31] In the biblical account, Moses received his name from Pharaoh's daughter (Exod 2:10); however, the text states that

---

29. The numerous uses of "Mary" in the NT implies a strong connection to the passing on of the name "Miriam"

30. Author's translation. Hartmann, "Mose und Maria," 621.

31. "Es kann im Deutschen übersetzt werden mit dem Partizip ('Von Ra geboren, gezeugt') oder nom inal ('Kind des Ra') oder auch als Verhalsatz ('Ra hat geboren'; deutlich im PNR c-ms-sw 'Ra hat ihn geboren'). Im Namen 'Mose' kann das ägypt. theophore Element im Umfeld eines israelitischen Monotheismus natürlicherweise weggefallen sein." Hartmann, "Mose und Maria," 617.

Pharaoh's daughter named him "Moses" because she "drew him out of the water." The Hebrew name *Mōšeh* derives from the Hebrew term "to draw out" (*māšâ*), but Pharaoh's daughter is not Hebrew, nor would it make sense for her to name the child a Hebrew name, though she recognized the child as a Hebrew when she discovered him (cf. Exod 2:6). The written record of Exod 2:10 seems to have translated what Pharaoh's daughter said into Hebrew by finding a Hebrew verb with the same vocalization as the Egyptian name. Hamilton suggests that the name *Mōšeh* is a pun based on assonance, explaining that "the name is explained not because Moses is derived from *māšâ* but because it resembles it in sound."[32]

Space does not allow for a fuller analysis of the names Assir, "Phineas," "Hophni," "Merari," "Hur," "Hori," and "Pashḥur"—all of which possess Egyptian etymologies.[33] Admittedly, whether the Israelites accepted the religious implications of the names cannot concretely be known.[34] Names reflect cultural identity. Even today, the name "Haruto" or "Mohammed" implies a cultural tie different from the name "Billy" or "Robert." The use of Egyptian names in Israelite genealogies demonstrates a degree of Egyptian assimilation.

## Secret Names

Names in the ANE signified personality and power.[35] Deities often possessed multiple names and titles. Trachtenberg notes how the phenomenon of a deity having secret names extended to the average Egyptian person:

> The members of many primitive tribes have two names, one for public use, the other jealously concealed, known only to the man who bears it. Even the immediate members of the family never learn what it is; if an enemy

---

32. See Hamilton, "מֹשֶׁה," *TWOT* 2:1254.

33. Hoffmeier, *Ancient Israel in Sinai*, 226.

34. Most Egyptianized Hebrew names belong to members of the Levitical tribe.

35. Wilson, "God and His Unknown Name," 12.

should discover it, its bearer's life is forfeit. In highest antiquity peoples, the occult power that inheres in the name is recognized, and the name itself is known to be a mighty and awesome force in the hands of the magician.... The more such names a magician has garnered, the greater the number of spirits that are subject to his call and command.[36]

Egyptian deities often possessed several names including a secret name known only to the deity. For example, some seventy-five names for the sun god Ra appear in the tomb of Thutmosis III. Because Ra had multiple names, Ra also had multiple *kas*, i.e., different emanations of the god given to humans. Each of these names was a demonstration of the forms of Ra and of the power he exerted.[37] Jan Assmann observes, "'Name' refers not only to proper names such as Osiris and Amun but denotes everything that may be said and told about a deity in epithets, titles, pedigrees, genealogies, myths—in short, its entire linguistic representation."[38] The name of a deity contained every aspect of power and control that the god could exert.

Secret names played a crucial role in attaining eternal life. The knowledge and utterance of secret names in the underworld enabled the deceased to navigate its perilous realms, gain favor from deities, and defend against malevolent forces.[39] The *Book of the Dead* contains numerous references to secret names as a means of ensuring a successful journey into the afterlife.[40] The opening hymn to Osiris speaks of his hidden forms and Maat as a hidden soul:

> Homage to thee, Osiris, Lord of eternity, King of the Gods, whose names are manifold, whose forms are holy, thou being of hidden form in the temples, whose Ka is

---

36. Trachtenberg, *Jewish Magic and Superstition*, 79–80.
37. See Huffmon, "Name," 610; see also Ringgren, *Word and Wisdom*, 43–44.
38. Assmann, *Of God and Gods*, 10.
39. Quirke, *Cult of Ra*, 29.
40. Wasserman and Von Dassow, *Egyptian Book of the Dead*, 101.

holy. Thou art the governor of Tattu (Busiris), and also the mighty one in Sekhem (Letopolis). Thou art the Lord to whom praises are ascribed in the nome of Ati, thou art the Prince of divine food in Anu. Thou art the Lord who is commemorated in Maati, the Hidden Soul, the Lord of Qerrt (Elephantine), the Ruler supreme in White Wall (Memphis). Thou art the Soul of Ra, his own body, and hast thy place of rest in Henensu (Herakleopolis). Thou art the beneficent one, and art praised in Nart. Thou makest thy soul to be raised up. Thou art the Lord of the Great House in Khemenu (Hermopolis). Thou art the mighty one of victories in Shas-hetep, the Lord of eternity, the Governor of Abydos. The path of his throne is in Ta-tcheser (a part of Abydos). Thy name is established in the mouths of men. Thou art the substance of Two Lands (Egypt). Thou art Tem, the feeder of Kau (Doubles), the Governor of the Companies of the gods. Thou art the beneficent Spirit among the spirits.[41]

The presence of secret names in Egyptian mythology unveils a system of beliefs and practices intertwined with the ancient Egyptian worldview.[42] The secret names of deities represent their true essence.[43] The knowledge of a god's secret name granted power over them. For example, Isis poisoned Re in a ploy to know his secret name:

> Now Isis is a wise woman, more rebellious in her heart than a million men, more choice than millions of gods, more to reckon than millions of spirits. She was ignorant of nothing in heaven and earth like Ra, maker of what is under the earth. The goddess she decided in her heart to know the name of the noble god.[44]

Ancient Egyptian religious texts and inscriptions reveal instances of invoking secret names in rituals and incantations to gain favor

---

41. Wallis, *Book of the Dead*, 11–12.

42. The naming of a Jewish male child on the eighth day at his circumcision may reflect the superstition of not revealing a name until an appropriate time.

43. Ritner, *Mechanics*, 26.

44. Ritner, "Legend of Isis," 33.

or command the assistance of the gods.[45] Some see a connection to this practice when Moses asks, "If I go to the Israelites and tell them, 'The God of your fathers has sent me to you,' and they ask me, 'What is his name?'—what should I say to them?" (Exod 3:13). When Moses asks the name of God, he is asking for more than an identifying label. John Oswalt suggests that Moses is asking, "Who are you really?", implying Moses's ignorance of Yahweh's generic identity.[46] However, Oswalt's observation seems to ignore Moses's cultural context. Moses asks God's name because he foresees the Israelites asking, "Who sent you?", implying the question, "Which of the gods commissioned you?" Moses does not ask the question merely for his knowledge. God already revealed his identity to Moses in Exod 3:6 when he says, "I am the God of your father, the God of Abraham, the God of Isaac, and the God of Jacob." Moses knows that this entity is the deity of his Hebraic ancestry. When Moses asks the name of God, he is asking for God's secret name, i.e., his true, unhidden identity.

Moses does not ask for the secret name of God to receive power from or control over him. Moses anticipates a disbelieving response from his relatives; however, with the "secret name" of God invoked, the Israelites might believe they have unlocked some form of concealed divine power. Yahweh's response does not provide the secret name but serves as the ultimate revelation of who and what God is. He replies, "I AM that I AM" (Exod 3:14). Bailey observes that Moses asks for an identifying title to which Yahweh responds with *'ehyeh*, the first-person common singular form of the verb *hāyāh*. However, when Moses tells the people who sent him, he responds with third-person masculine singular form. The grammatical change may imply that the tetragrammaton is not a "name" but a description of the God of Israel who, based on this description, is superior to the gods of Egypt. His identity is his eternal nature which is unchanging and constant.[47] The first two

---

45. Frazer, *Golden Bough*, 199.

46. Ross and Oswalt, *Genesis-Exodus*, 311.

47. See Bailey, *Exodus*, 86–88. MacLaurin is helpful regarding the formation and origin of the tetragrammaton. See MacLaurin, "YHWH," 439–463.

commands provide restrictions on the divine name in which one should not appeal to or abuse the name, thus keeping the name secret.

The practice of changing names is prevalent in Genesis but less so in the narratives of Exodus and Numbers. When the character's name changes, the character's internal perspective changes as well. Pederson observes that the new name's meaning reflects the internal character of the person:

> The name is the appellation characterizing each individual soul. In so far it may be said that the name is part of the soul, seeing that it is possessed by it like the body, and everything wherein it manifests itself.... The most important feature about the name is, however, not its linguistic significance, but the association with which it is charged. It is understood quite literally that the name is the soul.[48]

If Pederson is correct, one might expect Moses or Aaron to undergo a name change as well. However, both characters retain their names throughout the narrative. The reason is twofold: (1) Moses and Aaron do not display a narrative shift in personality, and (2) Moses and Aaron do not serve as the foundation for Yahweh's plan in the same way as Abram/Abraham and Jacob/Israel. While Moses and Aaron carry out Yahweh's plan, their "seed" is not the material on which these entities rest, as is the case with Abraham, Isaac, and Jacob. To phrase it differently, both Moses and Aaron possess their character flaws until their literary conclusion.

## Clothing

Before the Israelites leave Egypt, they pillage the Egyptians by taking gold, silver, and clothing. This scene indicates significant implications concerning the Israelites' cultural mores at the beginning of the exodus. The account is as follows:

---

48. Pedersen, *Israel*, 245–52.

## The Influence of Egypt on Israel's Secular Mores

> The Egyptians were urging the people on, in order to send them out of the land quickly, for they were saying, "We are all dead!" So the people took their dough before the yeast was added, with their kneading troughs bound up in their clothing on their shoulders. Now the Israelites had done as Moses told them—they had requested from the Egyptians silver and gold items and clothing. The LORD gave the people favor in the sight of the Egyptians, and they gave them whatever they wanted, and so they plundered Egypt (Exod 12:33–36).

Upon their flight from Egypt, the Hebrews plundered silver, gold, and clothing from the Egyptians. Yahweh foretold of this plundering in Exod 3:19–22 and 11:1–3.[49] Bailey notes that the text emphasizes the Hebrews' ability to leave Egypt in a state of joy.[50] However, the issue here is not the motive behind the plundering but the specific objects that the Hebrews took. The items of gold and silver will later serve as the material for the golden calf in Exod 32 and as the material required to form the utensils in the tabernacle (cf. Exod 26).[51] The collection of precious metals—of which the Hebrews would not have possessed as slaves—foreshadows the construction of the tabernacle in the second half of the book of Exodus. The collection of these items answers the narratival question concerning where slaves would have received such valuable items.

While the metals serve a specific purpose later in the exodus narrative, the third collected item is odd. The collection of silver and gold allows the Hebrews to acquire what they do not have in their context as slaves. Conversely, the Hebrews collect clothing—something they would have already possessed. Regarding clothing in ancient societies, Garroway, Palmer, and Erisman note, "Dress is more than a material object. It is a means to understand

---

49. Scholars debate the ethical issues surrounding the "plundering" (*nāṣal*) of the Egyptians. For a discussion of the ethical issues surrounding the plundering narrative, see Houtman, *Exodus*, 382–86; Coats, "Despoiling the Egyptians," 450–57; Collins, "Evidence," 442–48.

50. Bailey, *Exodus*, 153.

51. Hamilton, *Exodus*, 193.

## Shedding Egypt, Becoming Israel

how society constructs and performs identity, both individual and collective."[52] If one applies this observation to the Hebrews, the request for Egyptian clothing implies a willingness to look Egyptian during the exodus.

Clothing reflects cultural identity. On the one hand, the plundering of clothing from the Egyptians signifies the "stripping" of Egypt, which served as the first phase in Egypt's demise against the long-oppressed Hebrews that will ultimately cumulate in the destruction of Pharaoh's army (Exod 14:23–41). On the other hand, the Hebrews surely possessed clothing prior to their escape. Why would they need clothing from the Egyptians? While Egyptian fashion did not place much emphasis on modesty, the Egyptians held their clothing in high regard.[53] There was little difference in clothing style between the Pharaoh and a common farmer.[54] Egyptian clothing varied depending on the season. Cotton served as the primary fabric resulting in a light and breathable garment, while wool composed other garments for cooler weather.[55] To be sure, Hebrew slaves would not have worn the lavish colors and heavily decorated garments of the Egyptians, although the base of the attire would have been similar.

Given that the exodus from Egypt to Canaan should have taken eleven days (cf. Deut 1:2), the Hebrews may have believed that the foreign powers in Canaan would surrender without a fight if they looked like the domineering world power. To be sure, Yahweh approved of the Hebrews plundering the clothing just as he approved of the plundering of silver and gold. The exodus narrative demonstrates that when the Hebrews use these gifts to serve Yahweh, the gifts symbolize a new beginning, but when they do not, they perpetuate the past with its idolatry and oppression.[56]

Though not often addressed in critical commentaries, the issue remains concerning how Pharaoh's daughter recognized the

---

52. Fox et al., *Body Lived, Cultured, Adorned*, 2.
53. Brier and Hobbs, *Daily Life*, 128.
54. Brier and Hobbs, *Daily Life*, 134.
55. Brier and Hobbs, *Daily Life*, 128–29.
56. Hamilton, *Exodus*, 193.

infant Moses as a Hebrew (Exod 2:6). Enns and Hamilton say nothing of the issue in their critical commentaries. At the least, Exod 2 places Moses in an identity crisis that will ultimately culminate in Moses's becoming Hebrew in Exod 4:24–26.[57] Ancient commentators suggest that she saw his circumcision, but this is not apparent in the text. Others suggest that Moses's clothing may have reflected his Hebraic identity. If this is true, there may have been more of a division between the clothing of slaves and the clothing of the Egyptians.

Another fascinating scene in the exodus narrative is when the daughters of Ruel (i.e., Jethro) tell their father about how Moses rescued them from unfriendly shepherds, saying, "An Egyptian man rescued us from the shepherds" (Exod 2:19). Just as Pharaoh's daughter identified Moses as a Hebrew beside a body of water, so too do the daughters of Ruel identify Moses as an Egyptian beside a body of water. When Moses fled from his Egyptian home, he did not leave his Egyptian identity behind. Admittedly, the text does not inform the reader as to how the daughters of Ruel identified Moses as an Egyptian just as the text is silent on how Pharaoh's daughter identified Moses as a Hebrew. It is possible that Moses may have spoken Egyptian to these women; however, a better explanation is that Moses's clothing and grooming style likely reflected his Egyptian culture.

The law of Moses presents two laws regarding clothing: (1) the prohibition against a mixed material garment (Lev 19:19; Deut 22:11) and (2) the prohibition against wearing clothing of the other gender (Deut 22:5). Mixed material (often cotton and wool or linen and cotton) composed the clothing of ancient Egyptians.[58] The command to not wear mixed material clothing denotes the shedding of an Egyptian cultural marker. More controversial is whether the Egyptians practiced cross-dressing or engaged in a form of gender fluidity. Discussions of Egyptian cross-dressing tend to revolve around the female Pharaoh Hatshepsut. Diamond notes, "There were several other leaders in the New Kingdom

57. Dozeman, *Exodus*, 84.
58. Wertz, "Unraveling," paras. 5–9.

who displayed non-binary gender identities, such as Queen Tiye, Akhenaten, Nefertiti, and Tawosret."[59] Hatshepsut had a mythical account of her birth. According to this story, Amun impregnated her mother, Ahmose, making Hatshepsut the daughter of Amun. Egyptian pharaohs had always claimed to be incarnations of the god Horus. Each king adopted the title "son of Re." Some scholars suggest that Hatshepsut was the first living ruler to claim to be the direct physical offspring of a major god. Hatshepsut took on the masculine role, giving the title "wife of Amun" to her daughter.[60] Some Egyptologists argue that Hatshepsut represented a third gender, indicating that she dressed like a man in daily life, but this seems to bring modern perceptions of gender into a content in which the idea would have been foreign.[61] While female pharaohs often wore the regalia of male pharaohs, the practice of cross-dressing among the popular level in Egypt is more difficult to analyze. Regardless of the degree to which it occurred, the practice of cross-dressing in Egypt demands some type of connection to the clothing prohibition in Deut 22:5. Though Yahweh approves of the plundering of clothing in Exod 3:22, it seems that Yahweh also views this Egyptian association as a thing to shed since he places laws on the Hebrews that would prevent them from wearing certain Egyptian clothing. As Garroway, Palmer, and Erisman suggest, clothing allows for an understanding of societal constructs and identity. The Israelites taking and wearing Egyptian clothing demonstrates a high degree of Egyptian acculturation.[62]

## Food

Food reflects cultural identity.[63] Egypt's foodway (a society's collection, production, and consumption of food) was predominantly

59. Diamond, "Hatshepsut," 168.
60. See Stiebing Jr. and Helft, *Ancient Near Eastern History and Culture*, 214–17.
61. Diamond, "Hatshepsut," 169–70.
62. Fox et al., *Body Lived, Cultured, Adorned*, 2.
63. Hasty et al., *Introduction to Anthropology*, 431.

bread, onions, beer, and fish. While written accounts and artwork aid in telling the story of a culture's foodways, anthropologists also use residue studies of traces of food and drink in pottery, baskets, and gourds, as well as stable isotope (radioactive elements found naturally in food) analysis of human bones and teeth in which they measure these isotopes to determine the diet of an individual and the environment in which they lived. These clues to ancient foodways can reveal a great deal about daily life.[64] Exodus 12:34 states that the Israelites left Egypt with food rations:

> So the people took their dough before the yeast was added, with their kneading troughs bound up in their clothing on their shoulders.

Exodus 12:39 adds,

> They baked cakes of bread without yeast using the dough they had brought from Egypt, for it was made without yeast. Because they were thrust out of Egypt and were not able to delay, they could not prepare food for themselves either.

When the Hebrews approached the wilderness of Sin, they express their desire for the food of their former captivity:

> If only we had died by the hand of the LORD in the land of Egypt, when we sat by the pots of meat, when we ate bread to the full, for you have brought us out into this wilderness to kill this whole assembly with hunger!" (Exod 16:3).

The desire for these foods during the exodus demonstrates the desire for the Hebrews to hold on to their assimilated lifestyle of Egypt. Additionally, Num 11:5 adds to the absurdity of the complaint by referencing the spices that would have been used in their meals. Even so, the narrator acknowledges the illogicality of the complaint since the reader would know that the food of slaves was far measlier than the complaint suggests. The people crave meat and bread, to which Yahweh responds by sending meat (quail) and

---

64. See Hasty et al., *Introduction to Anthropology*, 434.

bread (manna). Yahweh gives what the people requested, but he does so in a way that allows the shedding of Egyptian identity. Although the complaint is hyperbolic, it does indicate the type of diet held in Egypt—a diet offset by the restrictions in the law of Moses.

## Meat

An Egyptian scribe named Pai-Bes described the glories of the capital city of Ramses (biblical Ramses or Raamses) in the nineteenth century as a city overflowing with food:

> The Residence is pleasant in life; its field is full of everything good; it is full of supplies and food every day, its ponds with fish, and its lakes with birds. . . . Its granaries are (so) full of barley and emmer (that) they come near to the sky. Onions and leeks are for food, and lettuce of the garden, pomegranates, apples, and olives, figs of the orchard, sweet wine of *Ka*-of-Egypt, surpassing honey, red *wedj*-fish, of the canal of the Residence City, which live on lotus-flowers, *bedin*-fish of the *Hari*-waters.[65]

The above poem describes the plentiful food available in the capital city of Ramses. Of special interest here is the abundance of fish and poultry.

According to Herodotus, the Egyptians had three distinct categories of animals: (1) sacred animals that could not be killed, (2) sacred animals that could be killed, and (3) animals that were not sacred.[66] The Egyptians made no distinction between domesticated and undomesticated animals; they only understood what was sacred and what was not sacred.[67] For example, like many other ANE cultures, Herodotus notes that pigs were deemed unclean in Egypt. The myth in which Seth, the Egyptian god of wrath, disguises himself as a black pig and strikes the god Horus in the eye

---

65. For the entire poem, see "In Praise of the City Ramses" in *ANET*, 413–14.

66. Clutton-Brock, *Animals as Domesticates*, 53.

67. Clutton-Brock, *Animals as Domesticates*, 53.

## The Influence of Egypt on Israel's Secular Mores

seems to be the origin of the pig as an "abomination to the gods."[68] However, the degree to which this uncleanness impacted the one who was in contact with the pig is debatable. Herodotus stated that no spiritual harm comes to the one who encounters a pig. He can become clean by washing himself in the river.[69] Herodotus further comments on the relationship between the Egyptians and swine:

> Secondly, swineherds, native born Egyptians though they be, are alone of all men forbidden to enter any Egyptian temple; nor will any give a swineherd his daughter in marriage, nor take a wife from their women; but swineherds intermarry among themselves. Nor do the Egyptians think right to sacrifice swine to any god save the Moon and Dionysus; to these they sacrifice their swine at the same time, in the same season of full moon; then they eat of the flesh. The Egyptians have an account of the reason why they sacrifice swine at this festival, yet abominate them at others; I know it, but it is not fitting that I should relate it.[70]

While the pig is not a popular source of food in Egypt, the lower classes commonly consumed pork with no severe spiritual or ceremonial repercussions. *The Eloquent Peasant*, an Egyptian story dating to the Middle Kingdom (ca. 2030–1650 BCE), lists pigs with favorable food stock.[71] Youri Volokhine notes the role of swine in Egypt:

> The pig is clearly associated with a *bwt* aversion in the Middle Kingdom's Coffin Texts. The pig is also generally excluded from the tables of offerings, except in special ritual circumstances, in XXth Dynasty and then Ptolemaic texts. Obviously, pork provides a popular and very widely consumed meat, except that its association with lower value livestock keeps it out of higher class cuisine. The mythological bond between the male pig and the god Seth may also contribute to the animal eventually

---

68. *ANET*, 10.
69. Herodotus, *Persian Wars*, 335.
70. Herodotus, *Persian Wars*, 335.
71. See Petrie, *Egyptian Tales*.

being despised in the priestly world. Nevertheless, no recommendation for the shunning of the animal is attested in the priestly monographs or elsewhere. On the contrary, the sacrificial killing of pigs for Sekhmet is mentioned in Ptolemaic texts. Ultimately, it should be noted that explicit mentions of dietary restrictions are infrequent. The question of food is not decisive or central to obtaining ritual purity.[72]

The Egyptians viewed animals in connection with worship, piety, and myth.[73] The type of meat consumed depended on factors such as social status, availability, and religious considerations. Brian Muhs suggests that meat was a rare gift for the Egyptians.[74] Although the Egyptians considered the cow a sacred animal, beef was commonly prepared by roasting, stewing, or grilling.[75] This is likely what the phrase *sîr habbaśar* indicates in Exod 16:3. In addition to beef, sheep and goats were popular choices for meat in Egypt, appearing in various Egyptian recipes including stews and grilled dishes.[76] The Egyptians domesticated various types of poultry such as ducks, geese, and chickens for meat and egg production. Nile fish such as tilapia and catfish served as the main source of protein in ancient Egypt. In addition to domesticated animals, the Egyptians hunted wild game such as hares, desert ungulates, and birds.[77]

The above Egyptian diet presents three types of animals that are deemed unclean by the law of Moses in Lev 11:1–47: (1) pigs, (2) catfish, and (3) hares.[78] It is not surprising then to read that the

72. Volokhine, "Ancient Egyptian Food Prohibitions," paras. 1–3, 9.
73. Moazami, "Evil Animals," 300–1.
74. Muhs, "Ancient Egyptian Cuisine," 14.
75. Muhs, "Ancient Egyptian Cuisine," 13.
76. Muhs, "Ancient Egyptian Cuisine," 14.
77. Muhs, "Ancient Egyptian Cuisine," 15.
78. There are no food restrictions in Genesis. Though some see a dietary transition from Gen 1:30 to Gen 9:3 (i.e., vegetarian to carnivore), Wenham notes that there is nothing in Gen 1:30 that prohibits humanity from eating meat. Genesis 9:3 may then endorse the post-fall practice of eating meat rather than inaugurate the practice. Wenham, *Genesis*, 34.

## The Influence of Egypt on Israel's Secular Mores

Israelites crave the food—whether clean or unclean—that they had in Egypt. In fact, Num 11:5 clearly states that the Israelites craved the fish of Egypt. While this "fish" (*dāgāh*) may have been tilapia and thereby was clean, Nile catfish was the fish of choice in Egypt. Moreover, the term *dāgāh* is rather vague. At times, the term appears elsewhere in the HB to denote large fish, such as the monstrous fish that swallowed Jonah. However, other times, the term denotes small fish, such as those that died when the Nile turned to blood (cf. Exod 7:18). If *dāgāh* denotes catfish in Num 11:5, we may infer that the Hebrews ate foods that were deemed unclean in the law of Moses such as pork or catfish during their captivity as these were the foods of the lower classes.

Several explanations have been suggested regarding why these foods were prohibited. Some apologetic scholars argue that this was how God would ensure the health of his people. Others see connections of these animals with the dirt as connected with death. However, Yahweh states in Lev 11:45 why he commands that these meats are not to be eaten. He states, "For I am the Lord who brought you up from the land of Egypt to be your God, and you are to be holy because I am holy" (Lev 11:45). Bulmer notes the significance of cleanliness among the Israelites and within the law of Moses:

> Leviticus [emphasizes that Israel] must be "holy." This status required them to assert, both their separateness from, and their ethical superiority to, their neighbors. Their ritual practices and prohibitions could, therefore, not be expected to be symmetrical and complementary to those of neighboring peoples, following a classic totemic model.[79]

The connection of the dietary code to the Hebrew's liberation from Egypt represents another more-shedding moment. In the same way that the Hebrews could no longer wear certain types of Egyptian clothing, now the Hebrews could not eat the same types of Egyptian food. The Hebrews' craving for the food of Egypt is more

---

79. See Bulmer, "Uncleanness," 308.

than a narrative reflection on Egypt's prosperity compared to the poverty of the desert. The craving for meat reflects a desire to eat culturally defining food.

## Bread

Carol Meyers observes that bread and other cereal grains were arguably the most important nutritional sources in the biblical period. This hypothesis has been upheld more so in recent years as the hypothesis concerning the use of the bevel-rim bowl has shifted from being a ration bowl to being a bread mold. This is predominately based on similarities between the bevel-rim bowl found throughout Mesopotamia and the Egyptian Old Kingdom bread mold (*bedja*) which appears in tomb scenes, figurines, and facsimiles.[80] Bread was plentiful in Egypt as wheat dominated lower Egypt while barley was more prevalent in upper Egypt. Cereal grains also appear in Egyptian tombs as food for the dead in the afterlife.[81] But just as the Hebrews had meat when they left Egypt, the Hebrews also had bread, though the departure occurred so rapidly that their dough did not have time to rise (Exod 12:34). The transition from Egypt (i.e., the world's breadbasket) to the wilderness (i.e., barrenness) prompts the Hebrews to crave what they once had. The craving is not for tangible bread but for the feeling of fullness.

Unlike various types of meat, the law of Moses does not depict bread as unclean. There are no prohibitions of any grain types in the law of Moses. The only prohibition concerning bread in the law of Moses revolves around the lack of yeast during the Feast of Unleavened Bread (Exod 23:15). To be sure, this is not a grain prohibition but a prohibition on the ingredient used in breadmaking that causes the dough to rise. Bailey observes that the Feast of Unleavened Bread at the first Passover marked a new start for the Hebrews with the unleavened bread, representing the haste in

---

80. See Chazan and Lehner, "Ancient Analogy," 21; Meyers, "Having Their Space," 14.

81. See Leek, "Further Studies," 199.

## The Influence of Egypt on Israel's Secular Mores

their departure.[82] The leavened bread they so craved called their minds back to, as Bailey says, "the good ole days" of slavery in Egypt.[83] The removal of the leaven to commemorate their departure from Egypt makes this new food culturally identifying. In this case, unleavened bread serves as a new foodway for Israel.

### Alcohol

Though Exod 16:3 does not mention any type of beverage, Israel's dependence on wine as their source of alcohol demonstrates another shift from Egyptian foodways. Wine appears in several religious rituals described in the law of Moses. Wine served as a drink offering alongside burnt offerings (Exod 29:40), and wine was an integral part of the Passover meal (cf. Exod 12:8). Although the Egyptians consumed wine on occasion, beer was more popular.[84] The NET renders the term *šēkār* as "beer" in Deut 14:26 and 29:6, though other translations use the phrase "strong drink," "fermented drink," or "similar drink" to liken *šēkār* to wine (*yayin*) in that it is alcoholic.[85] The two passages from Deuteronomy noted above indicate the Israelites continued consuming alcohol in the form of both wine and beer. However, the law of Moses also indicates a transition concerning alcohol's place in Israelite culture. The law of Moses also placed restrictions concerning the consumption of alcohol for the priests. Priests could not consume wine or strong drink when they entered the tent of meeting (Lev 10:8–9) or while performing their priestly duties (Lev 10:9).

The law of Moses also prohibited the consumption of alcohol for those who took a Nazirite vow, stating that these individuals must abstain from wine, strong drink, and any product made from grapes (Num 6:1–4). *Nāzar* means "to consecrate oneself"; thus, a Nazirite is a "consecrated one." The term *yayin* ("wine") and *šēkār*

---

82. Bailey, *Exodus*, 150.

83. Bailey, *Exodus*, 185.

84. Maksoud et al., "Beer from the Early Dynasties," 219.

85. *HALOT* notes *šēkār* refers to an intoxicating beverage, likely beer made from barley. See *HALOT*, s.v., "שֵׁכָר."

("beer," "strong drink") appear together in Num 6:1–4. However, the NET renders *šēkār* as "strong drink" rather than "beer" as it does in Deut 14:26 and 29:6. The remainder of the prohibitions for Nazarites emphasizes abstinence from products made from grapes including its juice, raisins, its seed, or its skin. "Vinegar" (*ḥōmeṣ*) may refer to the souring of wine; thus, wine seems to be at the heart of the passage. *Šēkār* likely does not refer to beer alone in this context but indicates a catchall term for all intoxicating drink. Wine was more prevalent in Israel; thus, wine received the most attention in Num 6:1–4.

Though beer was more popular in Egypt, wine held a high place in Egypt's religious practices. Wine appears in offerings to deities, in aspects of funerary rituals, and in the mythology of Egypt's gods. However, in several mythological narratives, beer served as the means of intoxication for many Egyptian deities. Karim El-Gawhary notes how the Egyptian goddess Hathor became drunk and thus spared humanity from annihilation:

> According to the ancient Egyptian myth, the goddess Hathor decided to finish off the human race. She would have been successful, too, if not for the intervention of the god Ra, who ordered Sektet to mix beer with the mysterious dada fruit and some human blood. When Hathor arrived the next morning to wreak destruction, she found the land flooded with this tempting concoction. Unable to resist, she took one sip, and then another, eventually becoming so drunk that she no longer recognized human beings.[86]

The Israelites would have known these tales.

---

86. El-Gawhary, "Religious Ferment(ation)," 14.

Although the gods of Egypt can become drunk, Yahweh differs. There is no indication that Yahweh consumed the drink offering.[87] The drink offering consists of pouring approximately one gallon of wine on the altar as a sweet aroma to Yahweh (Lev 23:13). Yahweh does not drink the wine, nor does Yahweh become drunk. Leithart views the Israelite wine offering as a sabbatical act indicating rest and celebration.[88] In this way, Leithart suggests Yahweh drinks the wine to signify rest in the promised land. However, Leithart overlooks two issues. First, the drink offering appears with a burnt offering as a "soothing aroma" (cf. Lev 23:13). Yahweh does not consume the items; he smells them. Second, Yahweh never becomes drunk or has his judgment clouded. Yahweh's original sabbatical rest in Gen 2:2 did not require alcohol or an offering. Wine may symbolize rest and relaxation in the new land, but Yahweh does not require the consumption of wine to perform those acts with his people.[89]

The shift from the popularity of beer (though beer remained accessible in Israel) to wine presents a new foodway for Israel and thereby denotes another instance of more-shedding.

## CONCLUSION

The exploration of Israel's interactions with Egypt illuminates the cultural and social influences that shaped Hebrew identity during their period of enslavement and the subsequent exodus. The acculturation of Egyptian practices, including the adoption of names, clothing, and foodways, underscores the extent to which Israel absorbed numerous aspects of their host culture. Yet, the biblical narrative simultaneously emphasizes a divine imperative to shed these traits, which redefines Israel's collective identity. The degree

---

87. The verbal form נסך (*nsk*) indicates a pouring out usually as a drink offering, though Isa 40:19 uses the term to describe the process of idol casting. *HALOT*, s.v., "נסך."

88. Leithart, "Theology of the Drink Offering," paras. 1–9.

89. Poo, *Wine and Wine Offering*, 5–38, 147–68.

of acculturation is evident in names with undoubtable Egyptian etymologies and the acquisition of Egyptian goods during the plundering of Egypt. Through this examination, the interplay between assimilation and separation emerges as a central theme in Israel's journey from bondage to covenantal community.

# 3

# The Influence of Egypt on Israel's Religious Mores

THE HEBREWS WERE NOT holy when they left Egypt. Deuteronomy 32:17 states that the children of Israel had deserted the worship of Yahweh in favor of worshiping idols. In this context, these idols (*šēdîm*; often rendered "demons") must refer to the idol worship performed in Egypt. The need to create sacred space among the people demanded a holiness code in which Israel was unique in its philosophy and practice. Certainly, the Hebrews retained some sense of their Abrahamic religious mores. Yahweh did not need to explain who Abraham, Isaac, and Jacob were to Moses at the burning bush (cf. Exod 3:6). Debate continues concerning how and how much Moses knew about his Hebraic heritage. Unfortunately, this question cannot be adequately answered given the textual information at hand. However, what can be known is that Moses knew the important details concerning his Hebraic religious heritage. This does not imply that Moses did not know or that Moses rejected Egyptian religion in favor of Yahweh worship.

Regarding the religious views of Israel, Leon Kass helpfully views Israel as the anti-Egypt.[1] Kass suggests that to understand Israel, one must first understand Egypt but only insofar as Egypt

---

1. Kass, *Founding God's Nation*, 136.

contrasts with Israel.[2] To be sure, Israel and Egypt present stark contrasts to one another; yet, Kass misses the fact that these contrasting features are not immediate or ongoing during the period of Egyptian captivity and the subsequent exodus.

Craig Bartholomew notes that the period of the New Kingdom (ca. 1567–1085 BCE) demonstrates a rise in implicit and explicit theology.[3] Wilkinson further notes the increase in religious practices after Akhenaten's (1353–36 BCE) short stint of monotheism:

> If the Amarna Period can only be seen as a decisive downturn for the fortunes of most of Egypt's cults, the following Ramessid era was characterized by recovery and unprecedented growth. Rameses II . . . is credited with building more temples than any other monarch in Egyptian history.[4]

The increasing interest of religion and cult in Egypt during the late Bronze Age would have impacted the cultural mores of its residents, whether citizens or captives. The Pharaoh even had a religious duty since he served as a priest in addition to his roles as king, builder, and conqueror.[5] Moses's role as an Egyptian prince indicates that Moses also served in Egyptian religious rites and festivals, perhaps even in the role of an Egyptian priest.[6] This chapter demonstrates the influence of Egypt on Israelite religion during the exodus in two areas: (1) physical representations of deity and (2) priestly duties.

## PHYSICAL REPRESENTATIONS OF DEITY

Like most ANE cultures, Egypt was polytheistic. These gods often belonged to certain geographical areas typically represented

---

2. Kass, *Founding God's Nation*, 137.
3. Bartholomew, *Old Testament and God*, 213.
4. Wilkinson, *Complete Temples of Ancient Egypt*, 25.
5. Sauneron, *Priests of Ancient Egypt*, 32.
6. See Assmann, *Moses the Egyptian*, 211–12.

## The Influence of Egypt on Israel's Religious Mores

by temples to that god/goddess. Besides the brief monotheistic stent during the reign of Akhenaten (ca. 1353–36), there was no separation between cult and culture in Egypt.[7] Teeter notes how the religious worldview of the Egyptians impacted every aspect of their daily life:

> Any sort of contact with the world of the Egyptians silences one question, that of the existence and reality of these gods. Egyptian religion lived on the reality that gods exist, and this certainty pervaded all of Egyptian life. If we remove the gods from the Egyptians' world, all that remains is a dark, uninhabited shell that would not repay study. The gods are a part of Egyptian reality and hence are for us at the least historical realities that should be taken seriously.[8]

The heightened sense of religion in Egypt demands an exploration of Israelite perspectives on deity during the exodus event. Evidence suggesting the presence of a monotheistic religion in Goshen is lacking, though the prohibition to honor any other gods before Yahweh in the Decalogue (Exod 20:3) implies some sense of polytheism in Israel's background. For the Israelites in Egypt, the available evidence suggests that Yahweh was viewed as another, though lesser, deity. Before Yahweh could lead his people out of Egyptian bondage, he had to prove his power. Yahweh's statement in Exod 12:12 states that Yahweh was at war with the gods of Egypt. Pharaoh, the living embodiment of Osiris and the son of Ra, by losing his firstborn ultimately lost the son of a god, placing Pharaoh as merely human.[9]

Stein hypothesized that the Hebrews worshiped idols during their captivity in Egypt:

> Israelites probably had idols in their Goshen homes, divine seats for God or other deities, in the form of a serpent (an early representation of wisdom and power, used by Moses to impress the Israelites and Pharaoh); a young

---

7. Bartholomew, *Old Testament and God*, 214.
8. Teeter, *Religion and Ritual*, 197.
9. Friedman, "Upon all the Gods," 8–18.

bull (to which the people would quickly revert in stress); a decorated post; or the cherub (a hybrid of human, bird and beast). The First Commandment emphatically rejects worship of other deities, although it does not deny they exist, and it is the only one of the Ten Commandments for which punishment for violation is explicit. Nevertheless, reversion to idol worship was rapid and easy . . . Israelites accepted the reality of magic, human usurpation of divine power over the natural world, as a technology one could obtain.[10]

The sentiment of Israel's inclination to idolatry appears in Moses's pre-conquest speech. Deuteronomy 32:15–18 comments on the rebellious nature of the people that will continue into Israel's future:

> They made him jealous with other gods, they enraged him with abhorrent idols. They sacrificed to demons, not God, to gods they had not known; to new gods who had recently come along, gods your ancestors had not known about. You forgot the Rock who fathered you, and put out of mind the God who gave you birth (Deut 32:16–18).

Moses's song speaks of the Hebrews worshiping other gods (*'ĕlōhîm*). These *'ĕlōhîm* are in parallel with the *šēdîm* in v. 17. The *šēdîm* reflect the sons of God mentioned in Deut 32:8:

> When the Most High gave the nations their inheritance, when he divided up humankind, he set the boundaries of the peoples, according to the number of the heavenly assembly.

The MT reads *bĕnê yiśrāēl* ("sons of Israel"). A Qumran fragment has *bĕnê 'ēl* ("sons of God"), while the LXX reads *angelōn theou* ("angels of God"), presupposing *bĕnê 'ēl* or *bĕnê 'ēlîm* as the Vorlage. Most scholars suggest that *bĕnê 'ēl* or *bĕnê 'ēlîm* is the original reading. The MT assumed that the expression "sons of God" refers to Israel (cf. Hos. 1:10), while the LXX assumed the phrase refers to the heavenly assembly (Pss 29:1; 89:6; cf. Ps 82).

---

10. Stein, "Religion of the Israelites," 196.

The phrase appears in Ugaritic referring to El's divine assembly. According to the latter view, the Lord delegated the nations to his angelic host (cf. Dan. 10:13–21) while reserving Israel for himself.[11] To that end, one may interpret Israel's view of other gods as legitimating their existence. The hiphil imperfect third masculine plural verb *yaqni'ūhû* in Deut 32:16 emphasizes the rebellion. The context places the action of the verb in a future reality, prophetically speaking of the later nation of Israel. However, the syntactical function of the imperfect reflects a former reality that extends into the future. This former reality then reflects the Israelite's religious assimilation to Egypt.

Deuteronomy contains several passages that assume the existence of other gods.[12] Gay Robins notes that Hebrews did not recognize idols as merely inanimate objects:

> When a non-physical being manifested in a statue, this anchored the being in a controlled location where living human beings could interact with it through ritual performance. In order for human beings to interact with deities and to persuade them to create, renew, and maintain the universe, these beings had to be brought down to earth. This interaction had to be strictly controlled in order to avoid both the potential dangers of unrestricted divine power and the pollution of the divine by the impurity of the human world. While the ability of deities to act in the visible, human realm was brought about through their manifestation in a physical body, manifestation in one body did not in any sense restrict a deity, for the non-corporeal essence of a deity was unlimited by time and space, and could manifest in all its "bodies," in all locations, all at one time.[13]

Dick notes that ancient people made a distinction between the statue and the deity that took residence in the statue.[14] Morenz

---

11. For a defense of this view, see Heiser, "Deuteronomy 32:8," 52–74.
12. Heiser, "Does Deuteronomy 32:17 Assume," 140.
13. Robins, "Cult Statues," 1–2.
14. Dick, *Born in Heaven, Made on Earth*, 33–34.

## Shedding Egypt, Becoming Israel

comments on the difference between Egyptian and Israelite views on the relationship between gods and idols:

> The ancient Egyptians would have agreed that the material and the sculpture fashioned from it were inanimate; this is why they were given vitality by the ritual. But later, and precisely at the time when they came into contact with Israel and the Jews of the Diaspora, the deity was thought to be in the heavens and only to take up temporary residence in his image after the necessary rite had been performed.[15]

Both the Israelites and the Egyptians would have recognized these idols as having divine significance.

The golden calf narrative in Exod 32 applies the practice of animal idolatry to the worship of Yahweh by employing an animalistic representation of Yahweh. Exodus 32:5 states, "When Aaron saw [the golden calf], he built an altar before it, and Aaron made a proclamation and said, 'Tomorrow will be a feast to the LORD.'" Aaron identified the idol with Yahweh. Whether the Israelite people made the same connection is difficult to say. Scholars debate whether the golden calf reflects an Egyptian or Canaanite custom. Hess notes that the idea of the calf forming itself (cf. Exod 32:24) echoes the "opening of the mouth" ceremonies of the Mesopotamians. Hess goes on to say that the eating, drinking, and playing referenced in Exod 32:6 resembles the victory celebrations of Mesopotamia. However, Egyptian connections to the golden calf cannot be so easily dismissed since bull/bovine imagery appears in Egypt as a symbol of power, fertility, and maternity.[16] Sharps smooths the issue by suggesting that the Egyptians originally borrowed their bull imagery from the Canaanites.[17] Egyptian art depicts Egyptian deities in three forms: (1) human, (2) entirely animalistic, or (3) semi-human, i.e., a human body with an animal head.[18] Petrie suggested that what had long been understood as

---

15. Morenz, *Egyptian Religion*, 156.
16. Hess, *Israelite Religion*, 156–57.
17. Sharps, *Sacred Bull, Holy Cow*, 46.
18. Pinch, *Handbook of Egyptian Mythology*, 7.

## The Influence of Egypt on Israel's Religious Mores

"animal worship" seems only to be an understanding of the relationship that man had with animals.

> It is difficult to separate now between animals which were worshipped quite independently, and those which were associated as emblems of anthropomorphic gods. Probably, we shall be right in regarding both classes of animals as having been sacred at a remote time, and the connection with the human form as being subsequent. The ideas connected with the animals were those of their most prominent characteristics; hence it appears that it was for the sake of the character that each animal was worshipped, and not because of any fortuitous association with a tribe.[19]

Lions, baboons, snakes, hawks, and bulls held sacred status in Egypt.[20] The Egyptians believed the gods took the forms of these animals or possessed the animal.[21] Different animals appear in different regions of Egypt. For example, the sacred animal of Thebes was the ram because the ram is associated with the god Amon. The jackal was known to parade around cemeteries; thus, the jackal became revered as Anubis. The bull was sacred throughout both upper and lower Egypt, though the bull received special attention in Memphis.[22] Thus, the Egyptians worshiped different animal images based on their geographical setting.

Most scholars connect the golden calf to Canaanite religious mores rather than to Egyptian mores due to the Canaanite storm god Baal-Hadad often appearing either with the head of a bull, riding on a bull, or standing beside a bull.[23] The legend of Baal-Hadad and Mot (the Canaanite god of death) parallels the destruction of the golden calf in Exod 32:15–20. In the Canaanite story, Baal-Hadad's consort Anat kills Mot. His body is burned with fire, ground up by millstones, and is left to be eaten by the birds. Though the

---

19. Petrie, *Religion of Ancient Egypt*, 21.

20. Lions adorn Pharaoh's bed and throne. The baboon often denotes wisdom.

21. Petrie, *Religion of Ancient Egypt*, 22.

22. Petrie, *Religion of Ancient Egypt*, 21–25.

23. Coogan and Smith, *Stories from Ancient Canaan*, 174.

## Shedding Egypt, Becoming Israel

Exodus account differs in that Moses ground the golden calf into a powder and forced the people to drink it (Exod 32:20), similarities exist nonetheless.[24] Because connections of the golden calf to the Baal cycle is a recent phenomenon, further study must occur to link the golden calf to Canaanite worship practices.[25]

Ezekiel 20:8 states that the Israelites worshiped the gods of Egypt prior to the exodus event:

> But they rebelled against me and refused to listen to me; no one got rid of their detestable idols, nor did they abandon the idols of Egypt. Then I decided to pour out my rage on them and fully vent my anger against them in the midst of the land of Egypt.

Clearly, the Israelites were familiar with Egyptian idolatry. The degree to which the Israelites would have been familiar with Canaanite idolatry is less certain. Contra modern scholarship, Midrashic texts connect the image of the golden calf to Egyptian religion. For example, a late midrash describes the Hebrew people calling out for a god who is like the Egyptians' gods (*Pirqe R. EL* 46).[26] This is based on the claim that the golden calf was a statue of the Egyptian god Apis.[27] *Exod. Rab.* 16:2 records Yahweh telling Moses, "As long as Israel worships Egyptian gods, they will not be redeemed; go and tell them to abandon their evil ways and to reject idolatry." For the early Jewish interpreters, the gods of Canaan played a small role in the golden calf narrative. Instead, the golden calf narrative echoes the religious mores of Egypt.[28]

---

24. Loewenstamm, "Making and Destruction," 485.

25. Eakin, Jr., "Yahwism and Baalism," 409.

26. See also *Tg. Yer.* to Exod 32:5; *y. Sotah* 3:4, 19a; *Exod. Rab.* 9:49.

27. Assmann, *Moses the Egyptian*, 71–72.

28. The prevailing view among scholars is that Israel did not spend four hundred years in Egypt but came to the highlands of Canaan after fleeing oppression in other parts of Canaan. For this reason, scholars connect the golden calf to Canaanite myth. However, were the Israelites in Egypt for four hundred years, they would not have known Canaanite mythology, but they would have known Egyptian myth. The rabbis, assuming a connection to Egypt, view the golden calf as an Egyptian more. For more on the view of Israel's origins, see Dever, *Who Were the Early Israelites?*, 153–67.

## The Influence of Egypt on Israel's Religious Mores

Israelite art employs bull imagery in the temple but not to personify or depict any deity. The image of cattle and ritual lavers as water sources might mirror the association between a cow in ancient Egypt and the Nile River, though this association is speculative. Instructions regarding the fashioning of the tabernacle's laver precedes the golden calf episode (cf. Exod 30:17–21). Though the text is silent regarding whether bulls adorned the tabernacle laver, the laver in Solomon's temple rested on twelve bulls (cf. 1 Kgs 7:43). Twersky hypothesizes that the laver of the tabernacle also rested on the backs of bulls, which would have provided a mold for Aaron to use in producing the golden calf.[29] However, the text says that Aaron "fashioned" the calf. The verb *yāṣar* is the same verb used in Gen 2:7 for the formation of man. Aaron does not fashion the calf by a mold but instead forms the calf with a *ḥereṭ* (engraving tool). Some have suggested that Aaron likely constructed an inner structure of wood and plated it with the molten gold. The verb does not demand that the image was solid gold since the word also appears in Isa 30:22 for gold plating.[30] Even if the laver of the tabernacle rested on the backs of bulls and thus provided a mold, there is no reason to connect those images with the golden calf.

The golden calf narrative presents a situation in which the Israelites used imagery they had learned in Egypt to depict Yahweh. While the bull is common to ANE representations of power, the use of a bull echoes that of the Apis bull worshiped in Memphis. Were the golden calf related to Canaanite religion, one would expect the image to include both a man and a bull like that of Baal. However, the golden calf is merely that—an animal representation of a deity.

## PRIESTLY DUTIES

Several scholars have linked Israelite priestly duties and the operations of the tabernacle to Egyptian religious practices. Friedman

---

29. Twersky, "Examination of Aaron's Role," 58.
30. See NET note 14 at Exod 32:4.

argues that only the Levites were enslaved in Egypt while the rest of Israel was in the high country of Canaan. Friedman argues this allowed the Levites to take on the religious roles in Israel.[31] Hoffmeier is less forward but notes that Korah's rebellion seems to reflect a pre-Israelite priesthood existing during the Israelite's time in Egypt.[32] Hoffmeier observes the oddity recognized by source critics who suggest Korah's rebellion served to legitimize the Aaronic priesthood.[33] Some have argued for a pre-exodus priesthood in Egypt for which Korah may have been a religious leader. Such hypotheses advance due to the physical descriptions and the names of Korah and On as they parallel current information on the Egyptian priesthood.[34] The name *Kōrah* means "bald head." While this reflects an odd physical description for an Israelite priest who could not shave his head, Egyptian priests shaved their entire bodies. For example, the tomb of Inherkau, the "Foreman of the Lord of the Two Lands in the Place of Truth" in Thebes, depicts him dressed in priestly regalia with a shaved head.[35]

Hoffmeier observes that the Egyptian term *wʿb* meaning "pure" describes a lower class of priests who assisted in various duties but could not enter the holy of holies.[36] The *wʿb*-priests handled sacred objects, which may lend to their requirement for shaved heads like that of the *ḥm nṯr*-priest. Korah is a Levite (Num 16:1) in possession of censers and incense (Num 16:17–18). Korah's possession of sacred objects may reflect a charge to handle

31. Friedman, *Exodus*, 25–30.

32. Williams' article, "A People Come Out of Egypt," argues that a study of the Hebrew Bible demands a study of Egyptological data. Williams notes that such a comparative study must be cautious; however, the evidence of Egypt's influence on Israel is apparent. Hoffmeier has championed this approach particularly regarding the Pentateuch. See Williams, "People Come Out of Egypt," 231–52.

33. Hoffmeier, *Israel in Sinai*, 229.

34. The priest of On has a theophoric name, which employs the name of the patron god, Re. See Hoffmeier, *Israel in Sinai*, 230.

35. Herodotus, *Persian Wars*, 317. See Porter and Moss, *Theban Necropolis*, 421–24.

36. Hoffmeier, *Israel in Sinai*, 229.

such objects in Egypt without holding the honor of entering the holy of holies.[37] The rebellion of Korah may too reflect a desire to advance from *wʿb*-priest to *ḥm nṯr*-priest, which would be synonymous with the role of *kōhēn* in Israel. As Hoffmeier observes,

> One cannot help but wonder if Korah might not have been a priest in the tradition of the *wʿb*-priest and is pressing Aaron for a promotion that would give him the status of a *ḥm nṯr*-priest (כֹּהֵן in Hebrew) and direct access to the holy place.[38]

On (or Heliopolis) is the name of the Egyptian city that housed the temple of Re/Atum. Joseph's wife, Asenath, was the daughter of Potiphera, priest of On (Gen 41:45, 50; 46:20). Hoffmeier suggests the name of Korah's coconspirator "represents a direct connection between the Hebrews and the cult center at On and may explain why a man with the same name who is not a Levite would join a conspiracy against Aaron the priest."[39] If Korah and On served as lesser priests of the sun god in Egypt, they may have believed that they should serve as priests in Israel, too. Hoffmeier argues that to their minds they were already qualified to handle sacred objects, and, in the Egyptian priestly system, priests could advance in rank—something not done in the Aaronic system.[40]

Such a view is not without its problems. Hoffmeier's argument relies solely on linguistic connections. The name On does not demand a priestly connection. In fact, Hoffmeier forgets that most priests of On, like Joseph's father-in-law Potiphera, have a theophoric element on their name (i.e., *-ra* on Potiphera). On's name may have come from the location or time of his birth. There is no evidence from the text demanding that the name reflects a priestly function. Additionally, matters of bloodlines may have prompted the rebellion. Why does the Israelite priesthood fall to Aaron's line and not that of Kohath? Perhaps the greatest issue with Hoffmeier's argument is that the rebellion is against Moses

37. Hoffmeier, *Israel in Sinai*, 229.
38. Hoffmeier, *Israel in Sinai*, 230.
39. Hoffmeier, *Israel in Sinai*, 230.
40. Hoffmeier, "Egyptian Religious Influences," 29.

(Num 16:2). Aaron is only a peripheral target. Numbers 16:3 states Korah's problem. Korah believed that Moses viewed himself as superior to the rest of the community. In this light, Korah does not necessarily desire any form of elevation but for Moses to be reduced.

Hoffmeier suggests that the name Korah demonstrates an assimilation to Egyptian religious tradition by denoting Korah's baldness. The trend for Egyptian priests to be bald contradicts the law of Moses, which demanded that Israelite priests not shave their heads (Lev 21:5). Sklar connects the prohibition to shave one's head to pagan mourning practices, though he admits this may simply be a cultural practice of the Canaanites from which the Israelites must refrain.[41] Hoffmeier demonstrates how the Israelites employed Egyptian loanwords to describe the regalia of Israelite priests.[42] The priests in Israel were to wear linen *šēš* garments. *Šēš* is a pre-exilic term derived from the Egyptian term *šs*.[43] Second Chronicles 3:14, quoting Exod 36:35, replaces *šēš* with *bûṭ*. However, the term *bûṭ* is absent in the Torah.[44] The usage of *šēš* to describe tabernacle and priestly garments in the Torah suggests an early origin for the term. *Šēš* refers to the outer linen garment of the priests while *miknāsayim* refers to the priest's undergarments. *Miknāsayim* occurs four times in the Pentateuch and once in Ezek 44:18, all of which denote priestly undergarments.[45] Exodus 28:42 suggests that the purpose of this garment was to cover the sexual organs:

> Make for them linen undergarments to cover their naked bodies; they must cover from the waist to the thighs.

41. Sklar, *Leviticus*, 250.

42. "Religious" ties and "theological" ties are not synonymous. Here, "religious" refers to those aspects of cult ritual that do not reflect theology on their own. Additionally, loanwords and linguistic ties to Egypt cannot on their own denote a direct correlation between Egyptian and Israelite theology.

43. David, *Ancient Egyptians*, 136.

44. Hurvitz, "Usage of Šēš and Bûṣ," 117–21.

45. Linen undergarments appear in the tombs of Tutankhamun and Khaʿ in Deir el-Medineh. They are on display in the Egyptian Museum, Turin. See Reeves, *Complete Tutankhamun*, 154.

The Egyptian term for men's undergarments is not known; however, Hoffmeier hypothesizes that since the Egyptian term *kns* refers to the pubic region, the Hebrew term *miknāsayîm* may derive from this Egyptian term.

## CIRCUMCISION

Because Israelite religion takes its shape during the exodus, few have reflected on already established religious rites and their changes during the exodus. The practice of circumcision changes from its original Abrahamic context to a neglected and improperly practiced rite within the four hundred years of captivity. Joshua 5:2 states, "Make flint knives *and circumcise the Israelites once again*" (emphasis added). *Wĕšŭb* (qal imperative masculine singular) and *mōl* (qal imperative masculine singular) are not joined by a conjunctive *waw*. *Mōl* is the governing verb since the second verb in an imperative + imperative construct without the copula governs the clause.[46] *Šŭb* serves as an adverbial periphrasis meaning "again," denoting the repetition of a previously performed act.[47] Additionally, the term *šēnît* ("a second time") implies the act had been previously performed. But how can one be circumcised *again a second time*? While it is possible that "a second time" could refer to a former mass circumcision that occurred at the first Passover (cf. Exod 12:48), only the first generation partook of this Passover. Here, however, Joshua speaks to the new generation of Israelites who did not live in Egypt. The more likely interpretation is that both *wĕšŭb* and *šēnît* refer to a prior Egyptianized form of circumcision. This interpretation allows for the men to have some remaining measure of foreskin and places the "removing the disgrace of the Egyptians" in the context of the circumcision act.[48]

On the surface, this view is problematic since Josh 5:5 indicates that these men "had not been circumcised." At first glance,

---

46. Gesenius, *Gesenius' Hebrew Grammar*, 386.

47. Gesenius, *Gesenius' Hebrew Grammar*, 387.

48. The "disgrace" of Egypt echoes the "disgrace" brought by Shechem's desire to marry Dinah (cf. Gen 34:7).

the phrase *lō'-mālû* implies an objective absence of circumcision since *lō* most often denotes an objective denial of fact.⁴⁹ If *lō* denotes an objective denial of fact, the syntax of v. 5 emphasizes the contrast between the status of the men who left Egypt (i.e., the first generation) and the status of the second generation. This nuance has carried over into English translations.⁵⁰

| NET | Now all the men who left were circumcised, but all the sons born on the journey through the wilderness after they left Egypt *were uncircumcised.* |
|---|---|
| ESV | Though all the people who came out had been circumcised, yet all the people who were born on the way in the wilderness after they had come out of Egypt *had not been circumcised.* |
| NKJV | For all the people who came out had been circumcised, but all the people born in the wilderness, on the way as they came out of Egypt, *had not been circumcised.* |
| NASB (1995) | For all the people who came out were circumcised, but all the people who were born in the wilderness along the way as they came out of Egypt *had not been circumcised.* |
| NIV | All the people that came out had been circumcised, but all the people born in the wilderness during the journey from Egypt *had not.* |
| CSB | Though all the people who came out were circumcised, *none* of the people born in the wilderness along the way *were circumcised* after they had come out of Egypt. |

Table 1: English Renderings of *lō'-mālû*

Egyptian circumcision did not completely remove the foreskin. Egyptologists agree that male circumcision was practiced in Egypt from predynastic times, though little evidence about the

---

49. Williams, *Williams' Hebrew Syntax*, 143.
50. Italics added for emphasis.

operation itself is available.⁵¹ Sasson observes, "Whereas the Hebrews amputated the prepuce and thus exposed the corona of the penis, the Egyptian practice consisted of a dorsal incision upon the foreskin which liberated the glans penis."⁵² While the Egyptians believed that the body must be intact for use in the afterlife, circumcision was an exception. Megahed and Vymazlová add, "Even though depictions of circumcised men are quite common in Egyptian reliefs, paintings, and statuary, scenes of the act of circumcision are rather rare."⁵³ A bas-relief at Saqqara (ca. 2250 BCE) on a tomb wall of Ankhmahor, a high-ranking official during the sixth dynasty of Egypt, presents the earliest image of circumcision as a surgical operation in Egypt. Though Herodotus suggested that the Egyptians were the first to circumcise children, these images of circumcision present adult men undergoing the procedure.⁵⁴ The bas-relief presents a man restraining the one undergoing the procedure by holding his hands together above his head while a surgeon performs the operation. A second man also undergoes circumcision. Unlike the first man, this one does not require restraint. The hieroglyphs read, "Sever, indeed, thoroughly," to which the surgeon responds, "I will proceed carefully." The second section presents the words of the surgeon to the one restraining the patient, "Hold him fast. Do not let him faint." The assistant replies, "I will do as you wish." Scholars wrestle with the identity of these men since the hieroglyphs do not give their names or roles. Most believe that these men are likely the sons of Ankhmahor who must take on their father's role as a priest.

According to Herodotus, the Egyptians performed circumcision for hygienic purposes.⁵⁵ Because the rite of circumcision seems to begin with adult men rather than with infants, the ones

51. Megahed and Vymazlová, "Ancient Egyptian Royal Circumcision," 156.

52. Sasson, "Circumcision," 474.

53. Megahed and Vymazlová, "Ancient Egyptian Royal Circumcision," 158.

54. Dobanovacki et al., "Surgery before Common Era (B.C.E.)," 30.

55. Herodotus, *Persian Wars*, 319.

who experienced the procedure would have felt the pain of the surgery and would have vividly remembered the pain after the surgery. Additionally, their recovery time would have been difficult and lengthy (cf. Gen 34:25; Josh 5:8). The hieroglyphs from Ankhmahor's bas-relief prove that the pain of circumcision was so great that the one undergoing the surgery might faint as a result.

By circumcising according to Yahweh's requirements, the children of Israel had "cut off" their former Egyptian disgrace by bearing the mark of God's covenant people. If this second Israelite generation underwent an Egyptian form of circumcision, the author of Joshua would by no means accept this circumcision as a valid means of obeying the law of Moses or for the fulfillment of the Abrahamic covenant. Additionally, an Egyptian circumcision would have left some of the foreskin for Joshua to circumcise *again a second time*. The issue then is not that the new generation had not undergone circumcision at all but that the new generation had not undergone the proper form of circumcision. Joshua's re-circumcision sheds the religious mores of Egypt and readopts the Abrahamic covenantal code, allowing the Israelites to become a nation with their own law (the law of Moses), land (Canaan), and king (Yahweh).

## CONCLUSION

Parallels between Egyptian religion and Israelite religion are paramount. Scholars have addressed these parallels in greater detail elsewhere. This section has narrowed the scope to emphasize the religious mores that are shed during the exodus event. It is important that we remember that the existence of similarities in religious practices does not imply plagiarism. While animal imagery, the priesthood, and circumcision allow for the shedding of religious mores, the impact of Egypt was not so easily forgotten. The character of Moses reminds us of how difficult it can be to modify our behavior. It is to his example that we must now turn our attention.

# 4

# Was Moses *Really* an Egyptian?
## The Sources Weigh In

THE NARRATIVE OF THE HB presents a silhouette of biblical characters in which the reader can know the thoughts of and at times understand the motives and actions behind the thoughts of the character. However, the narrative typically presents the reader with only a glimpse of the whole even if that glimpse seems from the reader's perspective to be a clear representation of the character. D'Amico's observation of disnarration in the HB proves helpful here. Disnarration refers to the elements of a narrative that explicitly refer to that which does *not* take place. In HB narrative, the author keeps nonessential details to a minimum. Unlike Homeric narrative that looks ahead, HB narrative often looks behind.[1]

Biblical characterization is challenging because it is unpredictable and changing.[2] The Bible rarely offers any physical description of a character and seldom gives information regarding biographical details such as birth and early-life narratives. Rather, the focus of biblical characterization is the present reality of that character—what this chapter calls *now-actions*.

---

1. D'Amico, "What Is Not," 184, 188; see also Auerbach, *Mimesis*, 12.
2. Alter, *Art of Biblical Narrative*, 143.

Now-actions are those events, decisions, movements, and thoughts demonstrated by the character within a present scene of a narrative.³ If one likens the narrative to a wagon wheel, the hub is the now-action from which come the spokes of characterization such as internal thoughts, physical descriptions, and cultural milieu. The now-action interpretive method evaluates a scene as one unique piece of the metanarrative by combining historical-cultural and literary hermeneutics into one coherent lens. Thus, the reader is not concerned with the historicity of the character or with narrative characterization alone but with how these historical-cultural details impact the development of characterization and how the character impacts the narrative flow of the individual scene. Thus, to develop a wholistic view of the metanarrative, the hermeneutic process must connect the individual now-actions whether they agree or contradict.

Figure 1: Diagram of the Relationship of Now-Actions to Plot.⁴

The now-actions of the character emphasize the intentions of the author to persuade the reader to interpret the actions of the character based on the circumstances of the metanarrative. Thus, Alter's observation that "all the indicators of nuanced individuality to which the Western literary tradition has accustomed

---

3. Bartholomew pleads for such a hermeneutic. He writes, "We need an approach to the OT that integrates the historical with the literary and the literary with the historical." Bartholomew, *Old Testament and God*, 51.

4. The diagram is my own.

## Was Moses Really an Egyptian?

us—preeminently in the novel, but ultimately going back to the Greek epics and romances—would appear to be absent from the Bible" does not account for instances where the narrator assumes a detailed characterization.[5] To phrase it differently, Alter assumes that the Bible presents an absence of detail to which the reader must fill in the gaps even if only based on assumptions. For example, Philo and Josephus, the NT, and the church fathers develop a characterization concerning Moses's early life in Egypt that goes beyond the now-actions of the Mosaic narrative as it appears in Exod 1–3. These reconstructions seek catalysts (i.e., a motive provided by the cultural milieu) for the now-action that is itself the result of a deeper force within the subconscious of the character.

Moses is a murderer in Exod 2, a shepherd in Exod 3, a force of vengeance in Exod 32 and disobedient in Num 20. However, he is a prime example of a faith hero in Heb 11:23–29, Acts 7:20–29, and in Philo's *De Vita Moises* and Josephus's *Antiquity of the Jews*.[6] Thus, these commentators reconstruct—as best they can—Moses's time in Egypt and his leadership during the exodus, which leads to the Moses figure becoming increasingly important in the Second Temple period and thereafter.[7] While clues concerning his social and religious mores appear in a few cryptic texts, the narrative of Exodus does not expound on Moses's formative years in Egypt.[8]

---

5. Alter, *Art of Biblical Narrative*, 143.

6. Coats notes, "Heroic narrative typically enframes its story with some account of the hero's birth and death. . . . Heroic motifs include not only the threat to his life by the Egyptian pogrom, with the corresponding exposure that commits him to his fate, but also the irony that develops in the princess's decision to commit him to a Hebrew mother for his initial nurture." Coats, *Moses*, 43.

7. Beal, *Illuminating Moses*, 59–63.

8. This is comparable to the information concerning Jesus's early life. Information concerning the upbringing and formative years of Jesus is scarce. At best, the text presents an instance where Jesus at age twelve stays behind to learn at the temple (Luke 2:41–42). This narrative shows Jesus's realization about his mission, though his mission will not formally begin until his baptism. None of the Gospel authors describe details of Jesus's home, his physical attributes, or his formal education. Luke summarizes such things by stating that "Jesus increased in wisdom and in stature, and in favor with God and

## Shedding Egypt, Becoming Israel

The command to circumcise baby boys on the eighth day appears both in the law of Moses (Lev 12:3) and in patriarchal history (Gen 17:11). Moses clearly knew the command, but he did not keep it himself or enforce it among the second generation of Israelite males. Additionally, the discontinuity of Moses as faithful leader of the Jews in the NT against the characterization of a reluctant and timid person in the exodus narrative begs for an exploration into the development of Moses's characterization primarily during his formative years in Egypt. This chapter first explores the influence of Egypt on Moses's circumcision status and subsequently his view concerning circumcision as a rite by evaluating the now-actions of Exod 1–3. Next, this chapter evaluates the views concerning Moses's relationship to Egypt as described by the author of Hebrews, Stephen in Acts 7, Judaizing Christians in Acts 15, and in select extrabiblical sources. This chapter concludes by developing a characterization of Moses that addresses the now-action of re-circumcision in Josh 5:2 as influenced by Egyptian mores.

## THE INFLUENCE OF EGYPT ON MOSES IN THE HEXATEUCH

The biblical narrative offers little information concerning Moses's early life in Egypt. However, the now-actions of Exod 2 and the need to remove the "disgrace of Egypt" in Josh 5:9 provide insight into Moses's literary characterization. The now-actions of Exod 1–3 demonstrate a trifold cultural shift by which, given the circumstances of Moses's context, make the prior assumption less than persuasive. Moses's pre-wilderness *Sitz im Leben* is paramount

people" (Luke 2:52). Matthew says nothing of Jesus's childhood. Mark begins with the ministry of Jesus. John says nothing of Jesus's childhood but connects Jesus to God in the beginning. These authors discuss the now-actions of Jesus. Several scholars have recognized Jesus in Matthew as New Moses. The lack of information regarding their upbringing may lend to another Matthean stylistic tool to paint Jesus as the new liberator. See Brown, *Birth of the Messiah*, 110–19; Vögtle, "Die matthäische Kindheitsgeschichte," 153–83; Allison, *New Moses*, 140–45.

## Was Moses Really an Egyptian?

to his character development since he stands at the crossroads of three cultures: Egyptian, Midianite, and Israelite. Thus, an exploration of the impact of Moses's birth parents, Pharaoh's daughter, and Moses's Midianite family as cultural and religious influences on his identity is necessary to connect Moses's cultural mores to the lack of circumcision observance and enforcement during the exodus.

The now-actions of Exod 1 center on the activities of the Hebrew midwives and the tyrannical rule of the Pharaoh. Exodus 2 introduces Moses as born in Egypt to two Hebrew slaves during that time of persecution and infanticide (Exod 1:16).[9] Jewish tradition depicts Pharaoh's daughter as righteous and the rightful mother of Moses:

> The rabbis depict the daughter of Pharaoh as a righteous figure who did not follow her father's wicked ways, but rather converted and ceased worshiping idols. By miraculously rescuing Moses, she was inadvertently responsible for the redemption of Israel, for which she was rewarded with a new name, Bithiah (daughter of God), identifying her with the genealogy in 1 Chron 4:18. She was highly praised by the Rabbis, and the midrash includes her among the devout women converts and those who entered the Garden of Eden while still alive.[10]

The Babylonian Talmud asserts that although Jochebed gave birth to Moses, he is the son of the Pharaoh's daughter because she raised him.[11]

There is no evidence in the biblical narrative that Moses underwent circumcision as a Hebrew infant. Rabbinic tradition argued that Yahweh was a circumcised male. Therefore, the rabbis also viewed the heroes of the HB as being circumcised from the point of birth, thus not requiring the physical surgery. Concerning Moses, the rabbis believed his circumcision status was

---

9. The names of Moses's parents are not in the birth narrative. They appear for the first time in Exod 6:18–20.

10. Kadari, "Daughter of Pharaoh," paras. 1–3.

11. Soṭah 3:19b.

embedded and implied in the adjective *tōb* ("good," "beautiful") as a description of spiritual and moral perfection.[12] However, the author of Exodus only informs the reader of Jochebed's actions, not her character. That is, the text does not offer information regarding Jochebed's devotion to the Abrahamic covenant, nor does the text provide any insight into the religious devotion of Amram who likely would have been the one to circumcise Moses if the act occurred. At most, the now-action of Jochebed in Exod 2 presents a loving mother who makes an ample effort to ensure her child's survival. To that end, Exod 2 centers on the secrecy of Moses. Jochebed hides Moses in the house, in the *tēbāh* ("basket"), and in the reeds along the river. Circumcising baby Moses would undoubtedly cause a noticeable ruckus, which contradicts the thematic narrative of secrecy.

On the other hand, the words of Pharaoh's daughter in Exod 2:6 offer an argument in favor of Moses's Hebraic circumcision when she says, *mîyaldēy hāʻibrîm zeh* ("This is one of the Hebrews' children"). The text does not state how she knew Moses's Hebraic identity, but something physically noticeable must have separated Moses from the Egyptians. Dozeman suggests that the identification of Moses as a Hebrew is a literary device intended to separate the people of God from the Egyptians.[13] He adds, "The birth story of Moses is not intended to make Moses Egyptian, but to place him in Egyptian culture."[14] However, as explained in the previous chapter, all Israelites underwent a baptism of Egyptian culture. The daughters of Ruel described Moses as an Egyptian man (Exod 2:19), implying he retained his Egyptian likeness upon his flight from Egypt. The separation of cultures that Dozeman wishes to make cannot easily take place on historical-cultural grounds.

Pseudo-Philo's *Biblical Antiquities* states that Pharaoh's daughter saw the "covenant," implying that she saw Moses's

---

12. Glick, *Marked in Your Flesh*, 51; see also Eilberg-Schwartz, *God's Phallus*, 39.

13. Dozeman, *Exodus*, 84.

14. Dozeman, *Exodus*, 84.

## Was Moses Really an Egyptian?

circumcision, stating, "And when she saw the boy and while she was looking upon the covenant (that is, the covenant of the flesh), she said, 'It is one of the Hebrew children.'"[15] Unfortunately, better hermeneutical practices must admit that this interpretation reads too much into the text. It is more probable (and favors the text) that Pharaoh's daughter knew Moses's Hebraic identity simply because he was a baby hid in the reeds along the Nile. No Egyptian mother would do such a thing. The Nile was dangerous. Waterborne disease, crocodiles, hippopotamuses, and snakes made the Nile often associated with death (i.e., the gateway to the underworld) and rebirth (i.e., the flooding that brought irrigation). Though one cannot be dogmatic concerning how Pharaoh's daughter identified Moses as a Hebrew, the narrator's point is that she knew that Moses was a Hebrew, yet she spared his life and raised him as her own child. Pharaoh's daughter, like the midwives of Exod 1, is the hero of the narrative. The female triumphs amid the persecution of the masculine tyrant. Exodus 1 and 2 demonstrate how the weak stand strong in righteousness, which foreshadows the Israelite's successes and failures during the exodus.

Through the intervention of Miriam and the approval of Pharaoh's daughter, Moses nurses at the breast of his birth mother Jochebed until he reached the weaning age. Though the text does not say how long Jochebed nursed Moses, most scholars agree that this period lasted approximately three to four years while Jewish tradition lessens the duration to two years.[16] Admittedly, this provides another opportunity for Moses's parents to perform Moses's circumcision. However, if Moses's circumcision did not occur on the eighth day of his life as the Abrahamic covenant dictates (Gen 17:12), it is unlikely that Moses's Hebraic circumcision would have taken place during this time either.

Given Moses's early immersion into unmitigated Egyptian culture, the possibility remains that he underwent circumcision as an Egyptian rite. The first term in Exod 2:11 presents the preterite with the *waw* consecutive. Here, the term carries the nuance of

---

15. Pseudo-Philo, *Liber Antiquitatum Biblicarum*, 9:15–16.
16. Kadari, "Jochebed," paras. 15–20.

"when he had grown up," indicating adulthood or at the least a greater sense of maturation. Stephen's chronology in Acts 7:21–22 asserts that Moses spent forty years in Egypt before fleeing to Midian, implying that he went through puberty in the Egyptian royal house. Feldmann notes that his Egyptian upbringing provided the catalyst for Philo's depiction of Moses as the ideal Platonic philosopher-king:

> According to Philo (*Mos.* 1.5.23), learned (*logoi*) Egyptians instructed Moses in arithmetic, geometry, rhythms, harmony, metrical theory, and the whole subject of music, as these disciplines are attested in the use of instruments and in literary treatises and detailed descriptions of a more technical sort. Despite the fact that Philo here ascribes the education of Moses in these subjects to the Egyptians, it is surely striking that these are the very subjects, indeed in that very order, that Plato (Resp. 7.521C-531C) prescribes for the higher education of his philosopher-king.[17]

As an Egyptian, Moses would have learned Egyptian law, court proceedings, mythology, mathematics, science, and literature. Moses, therefore, was more than an adopted Hebrew boy. The narrator of Exodus wants the reader to perceive Moses as an Egyptian in all ways.

If we take Moses's Egyptian context seriously, we must now revisit evidence discussed in a previous chapter concerning the depiction of circumcision on the tomb wall of Ankhmahor at Saqqara. Admittedly, scholars know little about circumcision practices in Egypt.[18] However, the tomb wall of Ankhmahor provides insight to the practice during the Old Kingdom period. In a previous chapter, this bas-relief established evidence for the presence of a religious more of adult circumcision that did not remove the entire foreskin. Here, however, the bas-relief demonstrates that circumcision was performed to adults of priestly status. My concern here

---

17. Feldman, "Philo's View," 273.

18. Megahed and Vymazalová, "Ancient Egyptian Royal Circumcision," 158.

## Was Moses Really an Egyptian?

is not about how the practice was performed but how the practice might have impacted Moses as an adult, who, as a member of the royal family, fit into the priestly class.

Much of what we know about circumcision in Egypt comes from the writings of Herodotus, who claims that the Egyptians performed circumcision to infants for hygienic purposes.[19] However, the bas-relief of Ankhmahor predates Herodotus by a millennium and closer fits Moses's historical context. Thus, Herodotus can only tell us what he tells us and nothing more. Though Herodotus attributes the practice of circumcision to all males in Egypt, this practice seems to have evolved from a rite reserved for priesthood inauguration. Egyptian priests may have viewed the foreskin in the same vein as body hair since it is well documented that Egyptian priests shaved their entire bodies.[20] Given that adults (at least in the Early Dynastic period) were the ones who underwent circumcision, the ones who encountered the procedure not only felt the pain of the surgery but would vividly remember the pain after the surgery.

Admittedly, the now-actions of Exod 2–3 do not present Moses as either an Egyptian or Midianite priest. However, the sub-narrative necessarily places Moses in the periphery of these contexts since the Pharaoh served as a priest and Moses's father-in-law was the high priest of Midian.[21] Moses's status as an Egyptian prince suggests that he served in Egyptian religious rites and festivals in the role of an Egyptian priest following his pharaonic status. Thus, Moses may have undergone an Egyptian priestly circumcision like the men on the tomb wall of Ankhmahor. Not all find this view convincing. Peters suggests, "[Moses] grew up under the protection of the Egyptian princess, but himself conscious of his Israelite origin."[22] Peters correctly observes that Moses obviously knew that the Hebrew people were his people (cf. *wayēṣē'*

---

19. Dobanovacki et al., "Surgery before Common Era (B.C.E.)," 30. Herodotus, *Persian Wars*, 319.

20. Herodotus, *Persian Wars*, 319.

21. Sauneron, *Priests of Ancient Egypt*, 32.

22. Peters, "Religion of Moses," 105.

## Shedding Egypt, Becoming Israel

*'el-'eḥāyw* in Exod 2:11), but how familiar Moses was with his people's religious customs cannot be known from the now-actions of the text. Further, Moses's identity upon his flight from Egypt is clearly that of an Egyptian as referenced in Exod 2:19. Were Moses circumcised as an Egyptian in the same manner as the men depicted on the bas-relief, he would have both felt and remembered the pain from this surgery. The hieroglyphic statement that one of the men undergoing the procedure might faint from the pain indicates no sedative was used. As such, it is not difficult to understand why Moses would have neglected the practice or at the least not pressed it upon Israelite males during the exodus.

Moses's blatant disregard for circumcision appears first in Exod 4:24–26. The "bridegroom of blood" pericope continues to be the topic of much scholarly debate:

> Nearly every modern commentator treating the pericope of the "bloody bridegroom" in Exod 4:24–26 introduces it as one of the most curious and perplexing passages in the Hebrew Scriptures. Ancient commentators operating under different methodological and philosophical considerations still, in the main, saw the need to find causal connections between Moses' endangerment and his past actions.[23]

While the comments provided here cannot answer every issue the passage presents, based on the proposed perspective that Moses underwent circumcision in his teenage or early adult years, a new interpretive lens is necessary regarding Moses's neglect to circumcise his son. The variant readings of the MT and the LXX add to the interpretive confusion.

One point of contention is that the MT presents Yahweh as the one who is angry with Moses while the LXX presents this figure as the *angelos kuriou*. Much work has been accomplished in recent years regarding the identity of the *angelos kuriou* in the HB. At times, this figure is Yahweh himself, which allows the LXX to utilize this term for the tetragrammaton. At other times, the figure

---

23. Embry, "Endangerment of Moses," 177.

## Was Moses Really an Egyptian?

is only a messenger from Yahweh to the subject.[24] The LXX's use of *angelos kuriou* could depict either option. Thus, the identity of this figure remains vague.

The second point of contention impacts the present discussion more directly. Verse 25c of the MT states *Kî ḥătan dāmîm 'attāh lî*. On the other hand, the LXX reads *Estē to aima tēs peritomēs tou paidiou mou*. The LXX emphasizes the child's circumcision, stressing that Zipporah is the one who performs the rite. The MT is less clear concerning whether the circumcised subject was Moses or the son.[25] Some suggest the "bridegroom of blood" pericope refers symbolically to Moses's circumcision. However, one should dismiss such an overly figurative reading since the text clearly states that the son, not Moses, receives circumcision in this narrative.[26] Zipporah's touching of the foreskin to Moses's feet—here perhaps a euphemism for the genitals—may present a symbolic circumcision via the son's literal circumcision.[27] Even so, there is no evidence from the text to suggest that the bridegroom of blood pericope denotes Moses's circumcision.

If one takes Stephen's division of Moses's life into three periods of forty years literally, Moses is approximately eighty years old during this event.[28] While the text does not specify the exact age of the son, it is safe to assume that the son was at least an adult (perhaps approaching forty years old) when his circumcision took place. Zipporah clearly knew how to circumcise and possessed the necessary tools to perform the surgery, perhaps having assisted

---

24. See Malone, "Distinguishing the Angel," 297–314. See also Heiser, *Angels*, 57–73.

25. This son may be Gershom, but the text leaves the son's identity nameless.

26. See also Dumbrell, "Exodus 4:24–25," 285–90; Butler, "Anti-Moses Tradition," 9–15; and Kaplan, "And the LORD," 65–74.

27. See Durham. *Exodus*, 58.

28. The number "forty" has both literal and symbolic meanings in the HB. If taken symbolically, the number could represent a significant length of time or the fullness of an event. In any case, Deut 34:7 states that Moses was 127 years old when he died. This provides a nice number with which to divide Moses's life into three periods of forty years.

her father in Midianite prenuptial circumcisions.[29] Moses's son is born in Midian to the family of a Midianite priest. If Moses had assimilated to Midianite culture, his son was likely unmarried, and Moses was likely ignorant of the requirements for Abrahamic circumcision. The now-actions of the narrative suggest Moses left any knowledge or connection to his Hebrew ancestry behind.

Why is this scene important to the overall Mosaic narrative? Embry compares the "bridegroom of blood" narrative to the Balaam narrative of Num 22 since both characters (i.e., Moses and Balaam) encounter supernatural danger while they are on a divinely commissioned journey.[30] According to Embry, the "bridegroom of blood" pericope presents a supernatural endangerment intended to promote Moses as a bona fide prophet. While an interesting juxtaposition, Embry's interpretation is unconvincing. The Mosaic narrative does not unfold to allow for a literary comparison of the two events. It is also unlikely that the earliest readers of these narratives would have made such comparisons. It is more convincing that the purpose of the pericope is to illustrate how Moses, the one newly called to lead God's people, must first get his own household in order before he can lead the nation of Israel.[31] To put his household in order, Moses must keep the fundamental command of the Abrahamic covenant—circumcise every male in the household—even though fully upholding the command to the strictest letter of the law would have been impossible. The son's age is well over eight days; however, the circumcision takes place and relents Yahweh's wrath. A similar event occurs in 2 Chron 30:1–3 in which the people of Israel and Judah partake in the Passover feast in the second month rather than the first. The text explains that this was so because there were not enough priests and the people had not come to Jerusalem to celebrate at the appropriate time.

---

29. While the Midianites practiced circumcision, most historians agree that Midianite circumcision occurred prior to one's wedding. See Stuart, *Exodus*, 153.

30. Embry, "Endangerment of Moses," 196.

31. The same principle arises in the NT concerning the elders of the church (1 Tim 3:4–5).

## Was Moses Really an Egyptian?

Though the act does not align with the original command in Gen 17, Moses's household must put off their Midianite and Egyptian values and become truly Israelite. The scene foreshadows Yahweh's removal of "the disgrace of Egypt" from the second generation in Josh 5:2–9. In this sense, Yahweh rolls the disgrace of Midian from Moses's household via the circumcision of the son, who is a member of the second generation. In the case of the second generation at Gilgal, the Abrahamic covenant must be properly reinstated for the recipients to avoid Yahweh's wrath.

## UNWILLINGNESS AS A LITERARY ATTRIBUTE OF THE MOSES CHARACTER

The individual now-actions form a metanarrative in the Pentateuch that develop a coherent characterization of Moses. While the book of Deuteronomy ends with Moses's speech to the children of Israel, the metanarrative presents him as a less-than-ideal leader. Though Moses appears as a fearless leader of the Israelites in later Jewish and early Christian tradition, the now-actions of Moses in the Pentateuch present a character who flees from responsibility.[32] Whybray notes, "On many occasions the author makes a point of presenting [Moses] as a fallible human being."[33] He continues, "At the outset, Moses runs away after killing the Egyptian (Exod 2:11–15). Later he is full of self-doubt, believing himself to be unfit for the task of facing Pharaoh and leading the people out of Egypt."[34] The author of Exodus wants the reader to perceive Moses as a man with imperfections. For example, the narrative of Moses's call presents a man who is reluctant and unwilling. The disjunctive *waw* in Exod 3:1 (*ûmōšeh*) breaks the narrative of Moses's divine call in Exod 3 from Moses in Midian at the end of Exod 2. The qal perfect third masculine singular (*hāyāh*) with the qal active participle (*rōʿeh*) illuminates Moses's *Sitz im Leben*. Moses had a wife,

---

32. Nigosian, "Moses as They Saw Him," 339.
33. Whybray, *Introduction to the Pentateuch*, 139.
34. Whybray, *Introduction to the Pentateuch*, 139.

## Shedding Egypt, Becoming Israel

a son, a job, and a well-respected father-in-law. Moses's response to Yahweh's call, "Who am I that I should go to Pharaoh?" (Exod 3:11), emphasizes his reluctance to leave his current lifestyle and to submit to his divine commission. The narrative moves the reader to sympathize with Moses's desire to maintain his current setting.

Feldman observes the shift in the admiration concerning Mosaic authority and leadership in Philo's *De Vita Mosis*:

> Philo adds the editorial-like comment that after his marriage to Zipporah, Moses, in taking charge of his father-in-law's sheep, received his first lesson in leadership (*hēgemonian*), since, as Philo says, shepherding is a preliminary exercise (*progumōasia*) in kingship for one who is going to be in charge of the most tame herd of men, just as hunting serves to prepare men for a career as generals. Consequently, as he remarks (*De Vita Mosis* 1.61), kings, as a term of the highest honor, are called shepherds of their people.[35]

For Philo, every aspect of Moses deserved honor. However, Philo's image of Moses as a leader, philosopher, and king stands in stark contrast to Moses's character in the biblical narrative. Eyre expresses the consensus among commentators when he writes, "[Moses] was indisputably one of the greatest leaders of all time."[36] "Indisputably" is a loaded word—one that Eyre uses inappropriately given the evidence. Even when Yahweh presents Moses with supernatural signs (e.g., Exod 4:1–9), he remains hesitant to do Yahweh's bidding. Moses's words *šĕlaḥ-nā' bĕyad-tišlāḥ* ("send by the hand whom you will send") in Exod 4:13 forcefully asks God to send someone else, emphasizing his reluctance.[37]

The generation that left Egypt had little respect for Moses's authority. The captive Israelites believed Moses's commission (Exod 4:30) but refused to keep that faith once they had left Egypt (e.g., Exod 14:10–12). Moses's word, whether from Yahweh or not, did not bear much weight during the wilderness wanderings. For

---

35. Feldman, "Moses in Midian," 8.
36. Eyre, *Moses*, 5.
37. Gesenius, *Gesenius' Hebrew Grammar*, §155.

example, Exod 34:29–35 describes Moses's shining face and the veil that concealed it:

> Now when Moses came down from Mount Sinai with the two tablets of the testimony in his hand—when he came down from the mountain, Moses did not know that the skin of his face shone while he talked with him. When Aaron and all the Israelites saw Moses, the skin of his face shone, and they were afraid to approach him. But Moses called to them, so Aaron and all the leaders of the community came back to him, and Moses spoke to them. After this all the Israelites approached, and he commanded them all that the LORD had spoken to him on Mount Sinai. When Moses finished speaking with them, he would put a veil on his face. But when Moses went in before the LORD to speak with him, he would remove the veil until he came out. Then he would come out and tell the Israelites what he had been commanded. When the Israelites would see the face of Moses, that the skin of Moses' face shone, Moses would put the veil on his face again, until he went in to speak with the LORD.

Dozeman suggests that Moses's veil may have served as a tribal mask, but this is almost certainly not the case.[38] Moses veils himself at times between meetings with Yahweh. Exodus 34:30 states that the people were afraid to approach Moses after those meetings. Perhaps the veil served as a way in which to keep the problems of the people at bay since Moses's shining face prompted fear among the people. On the other hand, the veil hid the shine, implying that Moses did not want the people to know when he did or did not possess the divine glow.[39] At best, the children of Israel viewed Moses as their liaison with God, not as their spiritual or political leader, particularly after the events of Exod 32. Nathaniel Helfgot observes, "The failure of Moses to lead the Jewish people into the promised land constitutes a central tragedy of the second half of

---

38. Dozeman, "Masking Moses," 22.

39. The word *kāran* derives from the noun *keren* meaning a "ray of light" (cf. Hab 3:4). Something of the divine glory remained with Moses.

the book of Numbers and the book of Deuteronomy."[40] The task of leading the second generation falls to Joshua.

Moses's faintheartedness in the narrative adds another layer as to why Moses neglected enforcing circumcision among the Israelites. For Moses, other aspects of the law such as Sabbath took precedence:

> While the Abrahamic covenant affirms strongly the ethnic component of the identity, it is the Sinai covenant, with its sign of sabbath observance, that establishes the cultic-religious element as the congregation of Yahweh. This is also an eternal covenant, an institution that requires observances as the condition of participation.[41]

Bruce Kimball adds, "The uniqueness of the Sabbath arose from its grounding in Hebraic religion, which basically reversed the concepts of human action and time in ancient Near Eastern paganism."[42] The rabbis disagree. R. Yose says, "Great is circumcision, since it overrides the prohibitions of the Sabbath, which is subject to strict rules."[43] Circumcision and Sabbath share several similarities. Just as circumcision marks the people of Yahweh, Sabbath observance serves a similar purpose in that the people of God are the only ones who observe it. Further, both Sabbath and circumcision possess historical and literary ties to Genesis. Perhaps for Moses, the Sinaitic covenant replaced the Abrahamic covenant, allowing the Sabbath to supersede circumcision as the indicator of God's people.

The now-actions of Moses's life string together a characterization of unwillingness, reluctance, and apprehension. Though the characterization of Moses in the Pentateuch is not shy about presenting his flaws, over the course of history, interpreters—both Jewish and Christian—rework the now-actions of the historical Moses to present a fearless leader and lawgiver.

40. Helfgot, "And Moses Struck the Rock," 51.
41. Van Seters, *Pentateuch*, 184.
42. Kimball, "Origin of the Sabbath," 306.
43. For more on the rabbinical views of circumcision, see Glick, *Marked in Your Flesh*, 47.

# Was Moses Really an Egyptian?

## THE IMPACT OF EGYPT ON MOSES IN THE NEW TESTAMENT

The depiction of Moses in the NT is both surprising and incongruent. Statements regarding the "custom of Moses" appear contradictory to the now-actions of the historical Moses. Jeremias performed an extensive study concerning the figure of Moses in the NT, concluding that Moses is on every page of the NT, though he appears most forcefully in the Gospels and Acts as the lawgiver.[44] Jeremias views Moses as the ultimate authoritative figure, distinguishing between Moses as a mediator of the law and Moses as the creator of the law.[45] Such a distinction runs the risk of attributing divine authority to a human vessel.

The statements of the NT, whether from Jews or Christians, depict Moses more favorably than the Pentateuchal narrative. For example, Moses often appears in the NT as the hero of the Jews. This is the case in Acts 15:21 where the text states *Mōusēs gar ek geneōn archaiōn kata polin tous kērussontas auton echei en tais sunagōgais kata pan sabbaton anaginōskomenos*. Wilson suggests that the passage is vague, making a contextual interpretation difficult.[46] Savelle concludes that the passage emphasizes Jewish sensibilities to recognize Christ.[47] At the least, the passage demonstrates a high degree of respect and honor given to Moses in Jewish circles of the first century. Further, the author of Hebrews makes grandiose claims concerning Moses's time in Egypt which the now-actions of the exodus narrative do not support:

> By faith, when Moses was born, his parents hid him for three months, because they saw the child was beautiful and they were not afraid of the king's edict. By faith, when he grew up, Moses refused to be called the son of Pharaoh's daughter, choosing rather to be ill-treated with the people of God than to enjoy sin's fleeting pleasure. He

---

44. Jeremias, "Μωυσῆς," 848–73.
45. Lierman, *New Testament Moses*, 10.
46. Wilson, *Luke and the Law*, 2.
47. Savelle, "Acts 15:21," 717.

regarded abuse suffered for Christ to be greater wealth than the treasures of Egypt, for his eyes were fixed on the reward. By faith he left Egypt without fearing the king's anger, for he persevered as though he could see the one who is invisible. By faith he kept the Passover and the sprinkling of the blood, so that the one who destroyed the firstborn would not touch them. By faith they crossed the Red Sea as if on dry ground, but when the Egyptians tried it, they were swallowed up (Heb 11:23–29).

The consensus among scholars is that the book of Hebrews fits the genre of a sermon, and while the author is unknown, the audience seems to be those Jewish Christians who had reverted to the ritualistic and legalistic ways of Torah observance. If one accepts that Jewish Christians were the recipients of the original document (or at the least hearers of the original sermon), the lens through which one interprets the text must include a Jewish gloss.[48]

The author of Hebrews claims that Moses fled from Egypt because he "refused to be called the son of Pharaoh's daughter, choosing rather to be ill-treated with the people of God than to enjoy sin's fleeting pleasure" (Heb 11:24–25). For the author of Hebrews, Moses renounced his Egyptian heritage by his own virtue.[49] Ellingworth correctly observes that this notion does not appear in Exodus, though he dismisses the incongruity in favor of a theologically motivated author with a homiletical tone.[50] James Thompson provides an alternative view:

> According to Exod 2:15, Moses fled to Midian after he killed the Egyptian and then returned. His second departure was at the exodus (Exod 14). If 11:27 is a reference to the exodus, the author has reversed the sequence between the exodus and Passover (Heb 11:28). If he is referring to the departure for Midian, his statement that Moses went out not fearing the king (11:27b) is not

---

48. For a fuller discussion of these issues, see Ellingworth, *Epistle to the Hebrews*, 3–29. See also, Thompson, *Hebrews*, 6–10.

49. Ellingworth, *Epistle to the Hebrews*, 611.

50. Ellingworth, *Epistle to the Hebrews*, 611.

consistent with the report in Exodus that Moses was afraid (Exod 2:14).[51]

There is a third view that both Ellingworth and Thompson neglect. The transition from an oral society to a written society throughout the Second Temple period led to the rise of Jewish legend.[52] The tradition of Moses that began with the now-actions of the exodus narrative had transitioned to depict him as an infallible hero in many Second Temple texts, causing the nuance of the now-actions to change. One reason for this shift is that the Jewish idea of "obedient faith" takes its shape in the keeping of religious rituals such as circumcision, generosity, adherence to food laws, and Sabbath observance, most specifically during the Seleucid oppression and Maccabean revolt. The books of Sirach, Maccabees, Tobit, Judith, and Susanna (among others) present instances in which obedient faith manifests as one's commitment to the entire law. The author of Hebrews understands that the ultimate fulfillment of the covenant is dependent on one's willingness to obey Yahweh's commands. For the author of Hebrews, Moses is the demonstration of faith par excellence. Not only does Moses provide an example of faithful obedience for the book's audience, but he provides a type and trajectory for how one can serve God's covenant people. Thus, one might excuse the author of Hebrews for his exaggeration of the Moses narrative based on his homiletic purpose.[53] However, the picture of Moses as one who did not enjoy the pleasures of Egypt to the point where he rejected Egyptian culture because of

---

51. Thompson, *Hebrews*, 242.

52. That is not to say that the early Israelites were illiterate to the point of having no written documents. Jeremiah, for example, explains that Baruch recorded Jeremiah's prophecies (Jer 36:1–32). Additionally, the discovery of the curse tablet at Mt. Ebal convincingly demonstrates a phonetic alphabet during the time of Joshua. The point here harkens to John Walton and Brent Sandy's observation that Israel "was hearing dominant and that the main transmission of information took place in the oral world, not the text world." See Walton and Sandy, *Lost World of Scripture*, 30.

53. Hebrews has long been understood as a sermon based on its self-pronouncement as an "exhortation." The same term appears in Acts 13:15 for a homily. See Thompson, *Hebrews*, 11.

his piety contrasts with other accounts of Moses's early life that are found in the NT.

Stephen's pre-martyrdom defense in Acts 7 gives a detailed history of the life of Moses that presents information not found in the Pentateuchal narrative. Stephen's trifold forty-year division of Moses's life occurs nowhere in the Pentateuch; however, extrabiblical sources popular in the first century commented on the timeline of these events. Jubilees 47:2–4 presents a chronology for Moses's infancy:

> And Pharaoh, king of Egypt, issued a command regarding them that they should cast all their male children which were born into the river. And they cast them in for seven months until the day that thou was born. And thy mother hid thee for three months, and they told regarding her. And she made an ark for thee, and covered it with pitch and asphalt, and placed it in the flags on the bank of the river, and she placed thee in it seven days, and thy mother came by night and suckled thee, and by day Miriam, thy sister, guarded thee from the birds.

Some have noticed an interpretive bend based on the phrase *wayigdal Mōšeh*. For example, Marshall attributes Stephen's three-part division to an early Jewish interpretation of Exod 2:11:

> A crisis in the life of Moses came when he was forty years old. The age of Moses at this point is not given in the Old Testament, but Stephen's statement agrees with the opinion of some of the Jewish rabbis; the figure, therefore, is probably meant to be taken simply as a round number. "Forty" was the age at which a person had "grown up" (Exod 2:11).[54]

Whether the number "forty" is a literal or figurative representation of Moses's chronology, Stephen asserts that Moses spent time in Egypt as a child and young man, time in Midian as a middle-aged adult, and time in the exodus as an elderly man. Moses did not spend his early/formative years in Egypt sitting on the sidelines of Egyptian culture. Exodus 2:19 makes it clear that Moses assimilated

---

54. Marshall, *Acts*, 148.

into Egyptian life. Therein lies the discrepancy between Stephen's speech and the author of Hebrews' observation.

For the author of Hebrews, Moses rejected his Egyptian upbringing, refusing to be called (i.e., associated with) the son of Pharaoh's daughter. Conversely, for Stephen, Moses's Egyptian identity was a blessing. Stephen states, "So Moses was trained in all the wisdom of the Egyptians and was powerful in his words and deeds" (Acts 7:22). Stephen does not limit Moses's education solely to academics. Stephen's use of the term *sophia* broadens Moses's Egyptian upbringing beyond that of academia. *Sophia* implies philosophical training and critical thinking skills. This is unsurprising given the vastness of Egyptian wisdom literature. Given that Moses spent his formative years immersed in Egyptian culture, it is not difficult to infer that Moses would have known Egyptian wisdom texts.[55] For Stephen, Moses's Egyptian upbringing was honorable. As Marshall notes, "The statement that he was mighty in his words and deeds (cf. Luke 24:19 of Jesus) may seem to conflict with Exod 4:10, but we should not attach too much factual accuracy to Moses' own self-depreciatory remarks which were little more than a pretext for avoiding a task that he did not wish to under-take."[56] The discrepancy between the author of Hebrews and Stephen implies that interpretations concerning Moses's early life in Egypt belong to the intentions of the interpreter.

One final example of the shift in Mosaic characterization in the NT comes from the debate regarding the gentile's relationship concerning the circumcision to the law of Moses. Acts 15:1 states, "Unless you are circumcised according to the custom of Moses, you cannot be saved," which implies a connection between circumcision and Moses. Modern interpreters often align the statement "custom of Moses" as synonymous with the law of Moses. Circumcision in the law of Moses appears in three contexts: (1) the ritual marking of a Hebrew male child (Lev 12:3), (2) a prerequisite for partaking of the Passover (Exod 12:44–49), and (3) a metaphorical

---

55. For more on Israel's wisdom tradition, see Sneed, *Social World*, 305–7.
56. Marshall, *Acts*, 148.

description of spiritual purity (Deut 10:16; 30:6).[57] If the "custom of Moses" in Acts 15:1 refers to the law of Moses, forcing gentiles to become circumcised according to the fullest letter of the law would be impossible since these gentile converts were older than eight days. Additionally, the Passover had been replaced by the Eucharist, which did not require circumcision (cf. 1 Cor 11:23–34), and baptism replaced circumcision as a metaphor for spiritual purity (cf. Col 2:11–12).

The alternative option is that the "custom of Moses" refers to Moses as one who performed circumcisions or even as one who underwent circumcision himself. However, the text is silent regarding whether Moses performed a circumcision, and the text is silent concerning his own circumcision status. Circumcising "according to the custom of Moses" cannot in effect describe the literal customs of Moses since the gap in circumcision from those who left Egypt (Exod 12:48–49) and the new generation of Hebrews (Josh 5:2) demonstrates Moses's lack of circumcision enforcement. The depiction of Moses in the NT is that of one who is ethnically Hebraic and religiously Jewish. The now-actions of Exod 2–4 dispute this characterization.

## THE INFLUENCE OF EGYPT ON MOSES IN EXTRABIBLICAL SOURCES

After the Pentateuch, David replaces Moses as the central figure in Israelite history. The NT heightens the importance of Moses since Jesus was viewed as the prophet "like me from your fellow Israelites" (Deut 18:15). The Moses figure then becomes increasingly important in the Second Temple period and thereafter. Ben Sira depicts Moses as a glorious saint while Aristobulus attributes Greek philosophy (namely Plato and Pythagoras) to Moses.

---

57. Exodus 12:43–49 cannot be part of the original Passover command. It is likely that Moses inserted this material to offer extra information and commentary on the meal. Exodus 12:43–49 serves as a footnote to the tenth plague narrative.

## Was Moses Really an Egyptian?

Artapanus agrees, depicting Moses as the founder of philosophy.[58] Space does not allow for a complete analysis of the Moses character from all extrabiblical sources. The discussion here concerns the views of Flavius Josephus, Philo of Alexandria, and Gregory of Nyssa since these sources offer the most comprehensive views of Moses in their respective interpretive veins. While each source presents a historical retelling of the Moses character, each does so with his own presuppositional and theological lens.

### Josephus

Josephus describes the early life of Moses in his *Antiquities of the Jews*:

> Thermuthis therefore perceiving him to be so remarkable a child, adopted him for her son, having no child of her own. And when one time had carried Moses to her father, she showed him to him, and said she thought to make him her successor, if it should please God she should have no legitimate child of her own; and to him, "I have brought up a child who is of a divine form, and of a generous mind; and as I have received him from the bounty of the river, in, I thought proper to adopt him my son, and the heir of thy kingdom." And she had said this, she put the infant into her father's hands: so he took him, and hugged him to his breast; and on his daughter's account, in a pleasant way, put his diadem upon his head; but Moses threw it down to the ground, and, in a puerile mood, he wreathed it round, and trod upon his feet, which seemed to bring along with evil presage concerning the kingdom of Egypt. . . . He was, therefore, educated with great care. So the Hebrews depended on him, and were of good hopes great things would be done by him; but the Egyptians were suspicious of what would follow such his education (*Ant.* 2.9.7).

The character of Moses in Josephus's *Antiquities* parallels the mythological accounts of Romulus and Remus, Oedipus, Cyrus,

---

58. See Beal, *Illuminating Moses*, 59–63.

and Theseus, namely given the motif of a threatened tyrannical empire and the exposing of a baby who would bring rescue from this tyranny. This is not surprising given Josephus's Roman context. However, Westwood argues that these similarities exist only broadly. She states, "[A] methodology of close reading which focuses on the precise motifs and themes highlighted by Josephus, rather than the broad brushstrokes of the overall narrative, reveals a more complex picture than merely an attempt to ratchet up similarities for the sake of proving to a Greek audience that Moses is a familiar type of hero."[59]

Josephus fills in the gaps of Moses's early life beyond the text of Exodus by inserting various narratives including those depicting military campaigns led by Moses. Josephus says nothing concerning Moses's circumcision as a Hebrew baby though he places Moses as the Hebrew par excellence. Josephus states that Moses received an Egyptian education but asserts that this was necessary to develop Moses's capabilities to liberate the Israelites. For Josephus, Moses was never really an Egyptian. He retained his Hebraic heritage knowing all the while—even in his infancy—that he was a Hebrew. To be sure, Josephus does not deny the influence of Egypt on Moses. Rather, Josephus spins the reality to demonstrate the providence of God. In this way, Josephus seems to make a parallel between the narrative of Moses and the narrative of Joseph. For Josephus, Moses received an Egyptian education because that was the only way in which Moses could liberate the people of Israel. In other words, Moses had to know the Egyptian world so he could overthrow it.

Josephus states that Moses received training in Egyptian warfare and thereby obtained military success from his Egyptian military career (*Ant.* 2.10.2). For Josephus, Moses's Egyptian experience was unavoidable because God had ordained Moses to be the liberator of the Israelites from his birth. Thus, the call of Moses in Exod 3 involved God persuading Moses rather than calling him to the task:

---

59. Westwood, "Prophecies and Princesses," 66.

> But God persuaded him to be courageous on all occasions, and promised to be with him, and to assist him in his words, when he was to persuade men; and in his deeds, when he was to perform wonders. He bid him also to take a signal of the truth of what he said, by throwing his rod upon the ground, which, when he had done, it crept along, and was become a serpent, and rolled itself round in its folds, and erected its head, as ready to revenge itself on such as should assault it; after which it become a rod again as it was before (*Ant.* 2.12.3).

The most extensive addition to the Mosaic narrative in Josephus is his addition concerning the Ethiopian expedition (cf. *Ant.* 1.238–253). In this account, Moses leads a successful campaign against Ethiopia. Upon returning to Egypt, he faces assassination, which forces him to flee. Thus, Josephus avoids any discussion of the murder scene in Exod 2:12. Scholars recognize the connection of Moses and Ethiopia based on Moses's Cushite wife in Num 12:1. A similar account appears in the works of Eusebius of Caesarea who quoted the (now lost) work *Concerning the Jews* by third-century BCE Jewish historian Artapanus. Even so, it seems likely that the separate accounts drew from an even earlier, wider body of source material. Eusebius related some of Artapanus's words as follows:

> But Moses with about a hundred thousand of the husbandmen came to the so-called Nome of Hermopolis, and there encamped; and sent generals to preoccupy the country [of the Ethiopians], who gained remarkable successes in their battles.... [T]he people of Heliopolis say that this war went on for ten years. So Moses, because of the greatness of his army, built a city in this place, and therein consecrated the ibis, because this bird kills the animals that are noxious to man (*Preparation for the Gospel* 9.27.1–11).

The Ethiopian expedition bridges the gap between Moses in Egypt and Moses in Midian. It also explains how Moses took a Cushite wife. The story provides evidence both of Moses's virtue and of his role as one who will bring the Egyptians low (cf. *Ant.* 2.238).

However, the narrative seems to do the opposite as Moses seems to be helping the Egyptians.[60] Josephus shapes Moses as the destroyer of Egypt by being its savior first.

Josephus is a historian, not a theologian. For Josephus, God used Moses's Egyptian context to develop his leadership and militaristic capabilities to liberate the Israelites all while never asserting that Moses was ever truly an Egyptian. Josephus argues that Moses retained his Hebraic heritage, knowing his Hebraic identity even in his infancy. To be sure, Josephus does not deny the influence of Egypt on Moses. However, Egypt is only significant externally for Moses rather than being an internal marker of his fundamental characterization. Josephus depicts Moses as having extensive knowledge of Egyptian warfare because that knowledge was necessary for Moses to liberate the Israelites. In Josephus's mind, Moses had to know the Egyptian world so he could ultimately overthrow it.

## Philo of Alexandria

Philo of Alexandria (also called Philo Judaeus or Philo the Jew) sought to bridge Jewish thought with Hellenistic philosophy. He presents Moses as the ideal leader and the model of virtue as he attempts to appeal to Jewish and non-Jewish audiences who are familiar with Greco-Roman principles of wisdom. Philo employs allegory and philosophical interpretation to portray Moses as a universal exemplar of virtue.

Philo authored two volumes on the life of Moses. He adds a subliminal undertone to the now-actions of Jochebed and Amram in Exod 2. For Philo, keeping Moses for three months to spare his life was worthless if his parents still had to expose him. Philo further notes the emotional distress of Pharaoh's daughter prior to her discovery of Moses. When she discovered Moses, Philo states, "And, recognizing that he belonged to the Hebrews, who were intimidated by the king's orders, she considered how to

---

60. Westwood, "Prophecy and Princesses," 80.

have him nursed, for at present it was not safe to take him to the palace" (*Mos.* 1.4.15–16). Philo glosses over the issue of how she knew Moses was a Hebrew. In this regard, Philo follows the text of Exod 2:6 without adding or subtracting physical details of the baby Moses.

Philo comments extensively concerning Moses's Egyptian education:

> Teachers at once arrived from different parts, some unbidden from the neighboring countries and the provinces of Egypt, others summoned from Greece under promise of high reward. But in a short time he advanced beyond their capacities; his gifted nature forestalled their instruction, so that his seemed a case rather of recollection than of learning, and indeed he himself devised and propounded problems which they could not easily solve. For great natures carve out much that is new in the way of knowledge; and, just as bodies, robust and agile in every part, free their trainers from care, and receive little or none of their usual attention, and in the same way well-grown and naturally healthy trees, which improve of themselves, give the husbandmen no trouble, so the gifted soul takes the lead in meeting the lessons given by itself rather than the teacher and is profited thereby, and as soon as it has a grasp of some of the first principles of knowledge presses forward like the horse to the meadow, as the proverb goes. Arithmetic, geometry, the lore of meter, rhythm and harmony, and the whole subject of music as shown by the use of instruments or in textbooks and treatises of a more special character, were imparted to him by learned Egyptians (*Mos.* 1.5.21–23).

Given that Philo attempts to unite Judaism and Hellenism, one might expect additions to Moses's life to include Greek philosophy and mathematics as part of his education. Zurawski notes, "The value of a proper education was, for Philo of Alexandria, unparalleled. Philo took a maximalist approach to *paideia*. His ideal model of Jewish education would include training in the preliminary, encyclical curriculum, the study of philosophy, and instruction through the laws of Moses."[61] One might expect Philo to take such an approach with the hero of the Jews.

For Philo, Moses's Egyptian experience did not make Moses "Egyptian" per se but provided him with a well-rounded system through which he could think and lead. For Philo, Moses's genealogy is more important than his *Sitz im Leben*. Although Philo oversteps the bounds of the text, his passion for reading Scripture was genuine.[62] As such, he believed that it was his responsibility to "peer into each to unfold and reveal the things which are not known to many."[63] Thus, Borgen calls Philo's treatment of the biblical text a "rewritten Bible."[64] Damgaard notes, "Because of the complex composition of the work, there is no scholarly agreement as to whether the *Life of Moses* ought to be understood as a genuine biography or as a commentary on the biblical account."[65]

Philo's depiction of Moses's rise to kingship reads, as Borgen calls it, a "mirror for kings."[66] Scholars disagree as to whether this elevation to "king" in Philo's mind is good or bad. Some suggest that Philo understood Moses as God's vice-regent where others see Philo's description as making Moses the philosopher-ruler.[67] Philo aligned Greek wisdom and virtue with the patriarchal tradition of Abraham, Isaac, and Jacob. To do so with Moses is not surprising.

## Gregory of Nyssa

The church fathers admired Moses.[68] For many church fathers, Moses demonstrated faith in action by accepting God's call despite the difficulties of dealing with Israel. For the fathers, Moses

---

61. Zurawski, "Mosaic Paideia," 480–81.

62. For insight into Philo's devotion to study while also taking liberty with the text, see Sterling, "Interpreter of Moses," 415–35.

63. Philo, *Spec. Laws*, 424–25.

64. Borgen, *Philo of Alexandria*, 46–79.

65. Damgaard, "Philo's Life of Moses," 234.

66. Borgen, *Philo*, 199.

67. Borgen, *Philo*, 202.

68. Hall, "Moses," 82.

personified the hardships and hopes of the believing sojourner passing through the wilderness and progressing toward a new home, often traveling with faithless people. While the fathers understood Moses as a significant figure in the biblical metanarrative, they tended to view Moses only as the first phase in the broader narrative to which Jesus would be the ultimate figure.[69] Thus, the fathers viewed Egypt and the wilderness as a metaphor for the realm of sin and as a representation of spiritual tyranny from which one should flee.

Moses takes on a new characterization in the church fathers as a prelude to Christ (cf. Deut 18:15–19). Because they had to affirm the OT (in most cases the LXX) as authoritative for the church, the fathers also had to acknowledge that God specifically chose Moses to accomplish his purposes in history. At the same time, they had to argue that Moses's person and work were still the first stage in a broader and deeper narrative in redemption history. For the early church fathers, Moses's life pointed to the entrance of Christ into human history.[70]

The fathers' views on Moses's early life in Egypt are less apparent. The education of Moses according to the apologetic writings of the church fathers made him greater in wisdom than all the Greek philosophers.[71] Justin Martyr suggests based on Philo that Moses had training as a royal child in philosophy, art, religion, and warfare.[72] Origen indirectly summarizes Moses's place among the writing of the fathers when he writes that the words of Moses "were filled with the Spirit of Christ" (*Princ.* 1). That is, Moses introduces the idea of Christ and works as the pre-Christ figure.

Gregory of Nyssa presents the fullest account of Moses's life from the church fathers. O'Connell suggests that Gregory's work *De Vita Moysis* places Moses as the figure of Christian perfection, though to do so admittedly results in hermeneutical discrepancies

---

69. Hall, "Moses," 82.
70. Hall, "Moses," 82–83.
71. Wolf, "Moses," 102.
72. Wolf, "Moses," 102.

from the source to the interpretation.[73] On one hand, Gregory depicts Moses as facing a vertical journey of self-reflection and self-discovery in which Moses ascends into higher union with God. On the other hand, Moses presents a horizontal journey in which he exists as a part of the children of Israel who together journey to the promised land.[74] Thus, Gregory shapes Moses as a pre-Christ figure as well as a pre-Christian figure who is aware of the dangers of sin and acts righteously amid the sin of others.

Gregory summarizes Moses's early life following the narrative sequence of Exod 2 while adding his own commentary to fill the gaps of the narrative:

> Moses is said to have been born when the tyrant's law sought to prevent the birth of male offspring. Yet in his outward grace he anticipated the whole contribution which he would make in time. Already appearing beautiful in swaddling clothes, he caused his parents to draw back from having such a child destroyed by death. Thus, when the threat of the tyrant prevailed, he was not simply thrown into the Nile but was placed in a basket daubed along its joints with slime and pitch and so was given to the current. (This was recounted by those who carefully gave a narrative concerning him.) Guided by some divine power, the basket moved to a certain place along the sloping bank where it was washed up naturally by the lapping of the waves. As the king's daughter happened to come to that grassy bank where the basket washed up, she discovered him when he gave a childlike cry in the ark. When she saw the outward grace evident in him, the princess out of her good will immediately adopted him and took him as her son. But when he instinctively refused a stranger's nourishment, he was nursed at his mother's breast through the contrivance of his close relatives (*De Vita Moysis* 1.16–17).

---

73. "The advantages of using the figure of Moses as a model for Christian perfection seem to be modified somewhat by the exigencies of dealing with the myriad other incidents which occur in the course of the exodus and desert wanderings." O'Connell, "Double Journey," 301.

74. O'Connell, "Double Journey," 302.

## Was Moses Really an Egyptian?

Gregory capitalizes on Moses's supernatural alignment with his Hebraic heritage to the point where the milk of an Egyptian wet-nurse was unclean. Because Gregory follows the Alexandrian tradition (cf. Philo), he often blends the *historia* ("literal") and *theoria* ("spiritual") in his writings.[75]

Gregory says little about Moses's life in Egypt, though he does recognize that Moses received a "pagan education" and a "royal upbringing" (*De vita Moysis* 1.18). However, Gregory continues, "He did not choose the things considered glorious by the pagans nor did he any longer recognize as his mother that wise woman by whom he had been adopted, but he returned to his natural mother and attached himself to his own kinsmen" (*De vita Moysis* 1.18). It is unclear to which event Gregory alludes here, although this statement aligns with the perspective of Heb 11:24–27. Interestingly, Gregory speaks favorably of Pharaoh's daughter. Thus, Moses's return to his mother cannot refer to her nursing him as he had "left childhood." For Gregory, Moses's attack against the Egyptian supervisor proved that Moses never truly assimilated into Egyptian culture.

For Gregory, Moses offers an example for Christians because he always sought to meet God regardless of his circumstances:

> For this reason we also say that the great Moses, as he was becoming ever greater, at no time stopped in his ascent, nor did he set a limit for himself in his upward course. Once having set foot upon the ladder which God set up (as Jacob says), he continually climbed to the step above and never ceased to rise higher, because he always found a step higher than the one he had attained (*De Vita Moysis* 2.227).

Early Western theology was dominated with formulating the minimum requirements for salvation. However, Eastern theology, to which Gregory belonged, was more interested in the maximum potential of salvation. Rather than framing salvation as a thing to be either in or out of, Gregory frames it as a never-ending process.

---

75. Jenson, "Gregory of Nyssa," 533.

Thus, the Christian life does not merely parallel the life of Moses. Instead, the Christian life is Moses's life realized in the gospel.

## CONCLUSION

The depiction of Moses across biblical texts and later interpretive traditions reveals a complex and evolving characterization shaped by historical, cultural, and theological lenses. This analysis highlighted the significance of developing characteristics from individual narrative scenes (i.e., now-actions) in the Pentateuch where Moses is portrayed as navigating the intersections of Egyptian, Midianite, and Israelite cultures. Later Jewish and Christian traditions recast him as a model of faith and virtue. While these portrayals sometimes diverge from the Pentateuchal narrative, they serve distinct theological and homiletical purposes. The varied interpretations underscore the enduring impact of Moses's life. This interplay between text and tradition invites ongoing exploration of Moses's identity and legacy.

# 5

# Becoming Israelite
## Joshua 5:2–9 as the Final Stage of Shedding Egyptian Mores

THE RE-CIRCUMCISION OF THE second-generation Israelite men takes place forty years after the initial exodus from Egypt (Num 14:34; cf. Acts 13:18). Deenick suggests that circumcision ceased during the exodus due to the people's rebellious nature. Butler broadens the interpretation of *ḥerpat* ("disgrace") by suggesting that *ḥerpat* refers to the whole experience of Egyptian captivity. For Butler, the Israelite's entrance into the promised land reflects genuine freedom.[1] However, Butler ignores the now-actions of the re-circumcision narrative, namely that the second generation had not been properly circumcised in the wilderness. It is the lack of circumcision that provides the catalyst for Yahweh's pronouncement, not the experience of captivity. That experience was removed at the crossing of the Red Sea. Verses 4–10 of the Song of Moses makes this clear.

> The chariots of Pharaoh and his army he has thrown into the sea, and his chosen officers were drowned in the Red Sea. The depths have covered them; they went down to

---

1. Butler, *Joshua*, 59.

> the bottom like a stone. Your right hand, O LORD, was majestic in power; your right hand, O LORD, shattered the enemy. In the abundance of your majesty you have overthrown those who rise up against you. You sent forth your wrath; it consumed them like stubble. By the blast of your nostrils the waters were piled up, the flowing water stood upright like a heap, and the deep waters were solidified in the heart of the sea. The enemy said, "I will chase, I will overtake, I will divide the spoil; my desire will be satisfied on them. I will draw my sword, my hand will destroy them." But you blew with your breath, and the sea covered them. They sank like lead in the mighty waters (Exod 15:4–10).

The Song of Moses expresses that the freedom experienced by the children of Israel was only possible by the power of Yahweh. The song is a celebration of God's victory. If the experience of slavery remained on the people until the second generation, then God's victory over the Egyptians could not occur until the Gilgal narrative. However, the Gilgal narrative does not connect the disgrace of Egypt to the Egyptians but to the lack of circumcision among the Israelites.

Creach suggests the circumcision narrative denotes the removal of the penalties of the first generation:

> In Joshua's theological schema the wilderness generation never completely shook off the stigma of Egyptian bondage, because it was not willing to accept the freedom of land possession. The wilderness wanderers carried a disgrace they could not remove, since they had a "life sentence" that disallowed their realization of the promise of Canaan.[2]

The second generation born in the wilderness did not know about life in Egypt apart from their assimilation to Egyptian culture that remained during the migration. Therefore, it is difficult to understand how any "disgrace of Egypt" in terms of tyranny and captivity might still be upon the Israelites in the context of the exodus and conquest.

2. Creach, *Joshua*, 57.

## Becoming Israelite

The now-actions present Yahweh's command for the new generation of Israelite men "who had not been circumcised along the way" (Josh 5:7) to undergo Abrahamic circumcision according to the standard set forth in the Abrahamic covenant (Gen 17:9–14). As previously noted, the Egyptians practiced circumcision; however, they performed the rite to adolescent and adult males by making a dorsal incision in the foreskin which exposed the glans penis but did not remove the entire foreskin.[3] There are two points of contention between Abrahamic circumcision and the circumcision practices of the Egyptians: (1) the Egyptians adopted the practice of circumcising infants at a much later date than the Israelites and (2) Egyptian circumcision did not remove the entire foreskin as did the rite prescribed by the Abrahamic covenant. The now-actions of the book of Exodus present a people group who are ethnically different from but culturally assimilated to Egypt. This suggests, following Sasson, that an Egyptian form of circumcision replaced the prescribed Abrahamic form of circumcision (cf. Gen 17:12), prompting the law of Moses to specify the Abrahamic version in Lev 12:3. Therefore, the male children of the second generation must undergo Abrahamic circumcision—removing the entire foreskin—to become partakers in the Abrahamic covenant, which granted the land of Canaan to the Israelites.[4]

This chapter first explores the purpose and method of circumcision in the Abrahamic covenant as it defines Israelite identity in terms of "otherness." Having developed a foundation of Abrahamic identity throughout the patriarchal history in the Genesis narrative, an evaluation of Israel's time in the wilderness as the process of forming national Israelite identity is necessary. This frames Josh 5:2–9 as Israel's final stage of developing a national identity.

---

3. Sasson, "Circumcision," 474.

4. The curse of Canaan in Gen 9:25 foreshadows the conquest.

# Shedding Egypt, Becoming Israel

## PRE-ISRAELITE IDENTITY: WHO IS AND WHO IS NOT?

"Pre-Israelite" refers to those of the patriarchal tradition extending from creation to Jacob. "Pre-Israelite" is not synonymous with "gentile." Hebrews 11 acknowledges this by presenting a series of non-Jew (e.g., Rahab), pre-Jew (e.g., Abel, Enoch, Noah), and Jew (e.g., Moses) character studies. From this perspective, faith marks someone as belonging to the community of Yahweh. The issue is not whether these characters are historical. Instead, the author uses their narratives as an object lesson for actionable faith.[5]

The patriarchal tradition displays a cycle of a man who is married to a barren woman. This woman supernaturally becomes pregnant and gives birth to two opposing sons. Yahweh then accepts one of the sons as the one through whom the original Abrahamic promise will pass. Abraham, the first patriarch, married Sarah, a barren woman, and had two sons—Ishmael, the son of Hagar, and Isaac, the son of Sarah.[6] Isaac carried the covenant as the child of promise. Isaac married Rebekah, a barren woman who, through supernatural means, had two sons: Jacob and Esau. Jacob carried the covenant promise while Esau began his own people group following the pattern of Isaac and Ishmael. Jacob married Rachel, a barren woman, and, through the provision of God, had two sons: Joseph and Benjamin. In its earliest form, the title "Israel" speaks specifically of Jacob the patriarch and subsequently of his twelve sons and their lineage.[7] The twelve sons of Israel present the first

---

5. Erich Grässer suggests the author understands the time before Christ (particularly realized in Heb 11) as a time when God tested faith. See Grässer, *Der Glaube im Hebräerbrief*, 65–66, 79.

6. Abraham has other children besides Ishmael and Isaac (Gen 25:1, 4; 1 Chron 1:32–33). However, these are not pertinent to the covenantal narrative.

7. The name "Israel" means either "to strive with God" or "God fights [for us?]." The account of Jacob's renaming is as follows: "So, Jacob was left alone. Then a man wrestled with him until daybreak. When the man saw that he could not defeat Jacob, he struck the socket of his hip so the socket of Jacob's hip was dislocated while he wrestled with him. Then the man said, 'Let me go, for the dawn is breaking.' 'I will not let you go,' Jacob replied, 'unless you bless me.' The man asked him, 'What is your name?' He answered, 'Jacob.' 'No longer will your name be Jacob,' the man told him, 'but Israel, because you have fought with God and with men and have prevailed'" (Gen 32:24–28).

time in the patriarchal narrative where all the male descendants of a patriarch compose a united people group who share equally in the covenantal Abrahamic blessing.

Genesis 12:1–3 establishes the relationship between Abram and Yahweh from which the covenant and its sign will derive. For Yahweh, Abram's obedience to the original command of Gen 12:1 stands at the crux of their relationship. Though theologians have long stated that Abram immediately obeyed Yahweh's call, Abram does not obey the command to "leave his family." Instead, he took his nephew Lot along the journey (cf. Gen 12:4). The parenthetical statement signified by the disjunctive *waw* joined to the proper noun *'abrām* in Gen 12:4b (*wĕ'abrām*) indicates Abram's motivation to disobey Yahweh's command to "leave his family." Abram took Lot because, from his perspective, Lot served as his logical heir. To be fair, the call narrative of Gen 12:1–3 does not indicate that God would make Abram into a great nation via his blood lineage or that Sarai would ever be a mother. Genesis 12:1–3 presents the establishment of the relationship between Yahweh and Abram, where Yahweh blesses and Abram is blessed.

Yahweh solidifies his promise to Abraham by "cutting" a covenant with him.[8] This cutting of the covenant assures the promise given in Gen 12:1–3. Covenant language does not occur within the call narrative of Gen 12:1–3. Rather, Yahweh's words exhibit what he will do for Abram as the result of his election. The assuredness of the promise appears in Gen 15:17–21 in the form of the formal covenant. In contrast to the call of Abram in Gen 12:1–3 where the text presents no obvious reluctance or hesitation from Abram, Gen 15:2–3 characterizes him as impatient and doubtful:

> But Abram said, "O Sovereign LORD, what will you give me since I continue to be childless, and my heir is Eliezer of Damascus?" Abram added, "Since you have not given me a descendant, then look, one born in my house will be my heir!"

---

8. Debate abounds regarding the covenant of Gen 15:1–21. For an analysis of these debates, see Deenick, *Righteous by Promise*, 16.

## Shedding Egypt, Becoming Israel

Yahweh proves the truth of his promise by swearing an oath by himself (Gen 15:9–21). He does this by passing through a heifer, a goat, and a ram that had been cut in half along with a dove and a young pigeon. The imagery of passing between the divided animals allows Yahweh to assert, "May what happened to these animals also happen to me if I do not keep my promise." Steinmann observes,

> The splitting of all the animals except the birds, which were probably too small to split, was part of a ceremony that accompanied the pledging of a covenant. Such a ceremony is mentioned at Jer 34:18–19. It is also probably reflected in the Hebrew idiom for making a covenant: "to cut a covenant." When the parties to the covenant passed between the divided animals, they were pledging to keep the terms of the covenant. If they failed to do so, they were symbolically invoking the fate of the animals on themselves: they, also, would be cut in two. Since God would pass between the animals, and since God cannot be divided, Abram would have absolute assurance that God would keep his promise.[9]

Hamilton notes the similarities between the covenant installment and covenantal agreements in Mesopotamian contexts. The custom there is to signify the agreement by slaughtering an animal. The animal's death only serves as the finalization of the agreement. Still others suggest a metaphorical, even allegorical, reading, suggesting that the birds of prey are warring nations, and Abram's "fighting off" the birds symbolize the need for a king/leader to fight off foreign nations.[10]

Neither Steinman or Hamilton address the fundamental issue at the heart of the covenant narrative. The HB acknowledges that lying is outside Yahweh's nature. Even the pagan prophet Balaam recognized that "God is not a man that he should lie" (Num 23:19). Nevertheless, the now-actions of Gen 15 place Abram in a context where he does not yet know the fullness of Yahweh's theological

---

9. Steinmann, *Genesis*, 174.
10. Hamilton, *Book of Genesis*, 431–33.

attributes. At this point for Abram, Yahweh must be like the other deities of the ANE. Joshua 24:2 states that Abraham's father Terah was an idol worshiper, implying that Abraham came from a polytheistic society. The Israelites' proclivity to paganism remains at the forefront of the HB's metanarrative. As Sommer notes,

> Biblical authors inform us that a great many Israelites—at times, perhaps even most Israelites—were polytheistic. This is true for the period in which the Israelites wandered in the desert, which is described in the Books of Exodus and Numbers; it is true for the earliest period of Israelite settlement in Canaan, which is described in the Book of Judges; and it is true through the period of the monarchies described in Kings. The Book of Judges narrates a repeating cycle of polytheistic worship by the Israelites, followed by punishment by Yahweh, forgiveness from Yahweh, and further polytheism on the people's part. The Book of Kings puts tremendous emphasis on the polytheism of Israelites both north and south. Some kings (for example, Hezekiah and Josiah in the south, Jehu in the north) are portrayed as having been exclusively loyal to Yahweh, but quite a few (Manasseh in the south and Ahab in the north, to take two notorious examples) encouraged the worship of many deities in the temples they sponsored. Prophetic books dating from this era paint the same picture.[11]

These gods are tricksters and liars who throw dangerous tantrums. For example, Ishtar releases the Bull of Heaven against Gilgamesh and Enkidu when Gilgamesh rebuffs the goddess's romantic advances. Additionally, some gods can be evil while still retaining their divine status. For example, Seth, the Egyptian god of chaos, is not synonymous with the Christian version of the devil. Rather, Seth represents the barrenness of the desert and the chaotic uncertainty of life. If we understand Abram's view of Yahweh as influenced by his former pagan context, the cutting of the covenant allows Abram to understand Yahweh based on his holy nature.

---

11. Sommer, *Bodies of God*, 149.

Thus, Gen 12:1–3 presents the election of Abram while Gen 15:1–21 establishes God's covenantal promise with Abram.

Circumcision is the "reminder of the covenant between me and you" (Gen 17:11). At its core, the Abrahamic covenant is a promise for descendants and land. Abraham's seed (*zeraʻ*) is the raw material needed to form this nation. Circumcision is a visible mark on the organ involved in the act that will produce the fulfillment of the covenant. Glick suggests that circumcision served as a sacrifice since the circumcision of an infant employed the cutting of flesh and outpouring of blood from a subject who could not resist.[12] However, the HB never identifies circumcision as a sacrifice, and to align circumcision with the cut animals of Gen 15 ignores the purpose of the rite as a sign (*'ôt*) of the covenant, not the covenant itself. Though males are the ones who carry this sign in their flesh, sexual intercourse exposes the female to the sign as well. Admittedly, a gentile woman can obviously become pregnant. Thus, the woman's pregnancy can only serve as the completion of the sign's promise when connected to an Israelite man. Medieval Jewish rabbis resolve this issue in the *Zohar*, a thirteenth-century Kabbalistic midrash:

> He who lies with respect to the sign of the holy covenant which is inscribed on him as if he had lied with respect to the name of the King, for the name of the king is inscribed in man. . . . in what does the lie consist here? He spread out his hands to the other power and lied with respect to [the place of] this covenant. . . . For he who guards this covenant is as if he was guarding the entire Torah. And he who lies with respect to it is as if he had lied with respect to the entire Torah.[13]

The woman carries the result of the promise and gives birth to the fulfillment of the promise. Men and women bear a sign of the promise that is visible at certain times and involves the reproductive organs.

---

12. Glick, *Marked in Your Flesh*, 3–11, 17–18.
13. Wolfson, "Circumcision," 102–3.

Abraham, Ishmael, and the men in Abraham's house undergo circumcision, but these individuals are older than eight days and had already received their names unlike Isaac who is named and circumcised on the eighth day. Erich Isaac suggests that Abraham's circumcision symbolized his rebirth.

> Whether Abraham in becoming "a new man" also died symbolically is not clear. A "death" is possibly hinted at in the first covenant ". . . a deep sleep fell upon Abram; and, lo, a dread, even a great darkness, fell upon him" (Gen 15:12). This sleep, described as *tardēmā*, is considered a deathlike sleep. Both Jewish and Patristic exegesis have regarded sleep and death as a continuum.[14]

Isaac goes on to say that circumcision may represent Abraham's "rebirth" because he receives a new name on the day of his circumcision (Gen 17:5). However, Abraham is not the only one to receive a new name in the Gen 17 pericope. Sarai also receives a new name (i.e., "Sarah") and undergoes a significant physical change in the opening of her womb. On the other hand, there is no evidence to suggest that the slaves or Ishmael received a new name at their circumcisions, so one should not press this observation too far.

The role of circumcision among non-covenant carriers of Abraham's descendants remains a debated topic among scholars.[15] For example, Ishmael undergoes circumcision although he is not the recipient of the Abrahamic promise and is thirteen years old when he receives the rite (Gen 17:25). R. Eliezer's commentary on Gen 17 declares that the foreskin is more unclean than any other blemish. Thus, he suggests that these foreign men received circumcision to prevent Abraham and his descendants from becoming unclean.[16] Additionally, the text does not forthrightly inform the reader of the circumcision status of Esau, though Jacob passed the ritual of circumcision on to his sons (cf. Gen 34:13–17), implying that both Jacob and Esau likely received the rite according to

---

14. See Isaac, "Circumcision," 452.

15. For a detailed analysis of the issue, see Thiessen, *Contesting Conversion*, 2011.

16. Friedlander. *Prirkê de Rabbi Eliezer*, 203–9.

its fullest observance.¹⁷ The practice was later observed in Edom (i.e., Idumea), though with variations:

> According to a new reading of Josephus, *Ant.* 13.9.1 §§257–58, [the Edomites] too were circumcised in a way different from the Jews. Smith translates the passage as follows: "And of Idumea Hyrcanus takes the cities Adora and Marisa. And having subjugated all the Idumeans, he permitted them to remain in the land if they would be circumcised and consent to use the laws of the Jews. And they, from desire of their ancestral land, undertook to make the circumcision and the other way of life the same as the Jews." The Edomites practiced circumcision but not the way the Jews did.¹⁸

The command to circumcise males on the eighth day does not make Abraham, Ishmael, or the men in Abraham's household ineligible for circumcision, as Yahweh commands that these men receive the rite as well:

> Abraham took his son Ishmael and every male in his household (whether born in his house or bought with money) and circumcised them on that very same day, just as God had told him to do. Now Abraham was ninety-nine years old when he was circumcised; his son Ishmael was thirteen years old when he was circumcised. Abraham and his son Ishmael were circumcised on the very same day. All the men of his household, whether born in his household or bought with money from a foreigner, were circumcised with him (Gen 17:23–27).

Though Ishmael is not the child of promise, he must bear the sign of the promise. When Isaac enters the narrative, Abraham obeys Yahweh's command to circumcise Isaac on the eighth day (Gen 17:12, 19; 21:4), making him the first to receive Abrahamic circumcision according to the fullest standard of the covenantal command.

---

17. Steiner, "Incomplete Circumcision," 503.
18. Steiner, "Incomplete Circumcision," 503.

Genesis 34 presents circumcision as a practice observed by the Hebrew community and a requirement for those who desire to join that community. Some have connected Dinah's body to figuratively represent the boundaries of Israelite identity. Others argue that the circumcision of Shechem reverses the rape of Dinah by self-mutilation of the genitals.[19] Camp discusses the issue from a source-critical perspective:

> Dinah's story seems to inscribe the riddle of identity, with its heart in priestly discourse. It was the priests for whom circumcision had such an important and multidimensional symbolic value: a sign of fertility, kinship, descent and maleness, it defined the turf of identity. But it must also have been priests who perceived that it was not a sufficient identity marker, for Israel or for themselves. Any man, after all, could be circumcised. Circumcision was, then, a powerful but insufficient symbol, requiring reinforcement from other cultural forms.[20]

Each of these perspectives, however, are at best modern literary formulations, none of which are offered by the text.

The phrase *'im tihyû kāmōnû lĕhimōl lākem kāl-zākār* ("you must become like us by circumcising all your males"; Gen 34:15) demonstrates the reality that circumcision had transitioned from a mark of the covenant to a mark of a people group within three generations. The word *kāmōnû* depicts circumcision as the way in which an outsider becomes part of the covenantal community. Additionally, the explanatory use of the niphal infinitive construct *lĕhimōl* demonstrates that the act of circumcision is how they would become like the sons of Jacob.[21]

This short exploration of the institution of circumcision presents the theological contrast between Egyptian circumcision and Abrahamic circumcision as it appears in the Genesis narrative. Yahweh institutes circumcision as the sign of the covenantal promise to make Abraham the father of nations. Throughout

---

19. See Glick, *Marked in Your Flesh*, 25; Thiessen, *Contesting Conversion*, 50.
20. Camp, *Wise, Strange and Holy*, 301.
21. Williams, *Williams' Hebrew Syntax* §195.

subsequent generations, circumcision morphs into the identifier of Yahweh's people.[22] By removing the entire foreskin from the penis, both the bearer of the sign (i.e., the male) and the recipient of the sign's promise (i.e., the female) experience the sign within the procreative act. The adoption of Egyptian circumcision perverts the theological significance of Abrahamic circumcision.

## THE EXODUS AS IDENTITY FORMATION

Debate abounds concerning the date and circumstances of Israel's formation as a sovereign nation. Sherwood argues that the mixed multitude of Exod 12:38 defines national Israel by its worship rather than its genealogy.[23] However, Burrell argues, "The ethnic self can be imagined only in contrast to an ethnic other," implying the identity of national Israel must exist in contrast with other independent nationalized entities.[24] Bakon and Goodnick argue that Israel's national status begins as early as Jacob given that the text presents him in juxtaposition to Laban (i.e., the Aramean) and Esau (i.e., Edom). For Bakon, Jacob's settlement in Goshen (Gen 45:10; 47:1, 4, 6, esp. 27), while a temporary settlement, allowed his family to "continue its traditional way of life," implying the nationalistic identity of Israel begins with its namesake.[25] Goodnick argues, "The travels of Jacob with his family and followers portray the original transformation and development into a distinct people."[26]

Reflecting the perspective of more recent critical scholarship, Bloch-Smith argues that national Israel begins as early as the twelfth or eleventh centuries BCE based on a combination of

---

22. The book of Jubilees holds this interpretation of circumcision. In addition, the rabbis use circumcision to exclude the gentiles from the designation "sons of the covenant." See Hoenig, "Circumcision," 330.

23. Sherwood, "Mixed Multitude," 141.

24. Burrell, *Cushites*, 104.

25. Bakon, "Jacob," 42.

26. Goodnick, "Israel's Defining Experience," 192.

## Becoming Israelite

archaeological evidence with the biblical record.[27] For her, there is no Israel if there is no archaeological evidence to support the claims of the biblical text. Nevertheless, debate continues concerning the archaeological evidence. Halpern suggests, "It is from [the era of Deborah] that real Israelite nationhood in the institutional and ideological senses can be traced."[28] However, the term "nationhood" again presents issue. For example, does the moniker "Israel," "Israelite," or "Hebrew" denote national status? The term "Apiru" appears on an Egyptian ostracon. If this term identifies the biblical Hebrews, do these people deserve national status without land or law? Kitchen notes, "It has been suggested that the little-known Egyptian ostracon refers to the Apiru, engaged in construction work at the city of Pi-Rameses. It indeed mentions the Apiru, but simply as bringing together stones under Egyptian military supervision."[29] Thus, to what degree the Apiru refers to the Hebrews in Egyptian captivity remains a matter of debate for which space does not allow.

Another archeological artifact riddled in controversy is the Merneptah Stele, an inscription by the pharaoh Merneptah who reigned from 1213 to 1203 BCE. The majority of the text records Merneptah's victory over the Libyans; however, the last three lines describe a separate operation in Canaan, then part of Egypt's possessions. The stele raises scholarly attention in the field of biblical studies due to a hieroglyph that most scholars translate as "Israel."[30] The other cities in the conquest list include the determinative for a city (i.e., a throw stick and three mountains). However, Israel's determinative is the symbol for a foreign people (i.e., the throw stick and a seated man and woman). Thus, it seems that the Egyptians during the time of Merneptah did not view Israel as a sovereign nation. Conversely, the phrase *běnê yiśrā'ēl* ("sons/children of Israel") appears in the HB as an identifier of Israel during its united monarchy (cf. 1 Sam 7:2; 2 Kgs 17:6; 18:11). The description *bēyt*

---

27. Bloch-Smith, "Israelite Ethnicity," 402.
28. Halpern, *Emergence of Israel*, 241.
29. Kitchen, *On the Reliability*, 263.
30. Drower, *Flinders Petrie*, 221.

## Shedding Egypt, Becoming Israel

*yiśrā'ēl* ("house of Israel") appears throughout the HB as well, though most notably in Exodus—a context in which the "nation" (*bēyt*) of Israel did not formally exist.

Frank places the crux of the issue on the term "nation" rather than on the term "Israel." Frank rightly notes that the title of "Israel" can refer to a patriarch, a geographical territory, and an idealized community depending on its context.[31] "Nation" and "national," on the other hand, reflect a modern phenomenon that requires more than kinship and culture as essential elements.[32] Additionally, the terms "nation" and "ethnicity," though closely related, are not synonymous. Frank summarizes the issue:

> Nobody seems to have any problem ascribing ethnic traits to ancient groups, since all that does is characterize the group in a limited way that precludes having to deal with or explain an ancient nation or nationalism. But ascribing national traits to ancient groups immediately opens the inquiry to the problem of reconciling the existence of an ancient nation with the "broad consensus" of modernist theories that fail to explain ancient nations.[33]

In this light, Israel may at times fit the categories of "proto-nationalism" and "precocious nationalism" depending on its temporal context.

If kinship and culture do not define a "nation," defining "national Israel" must encompass specific criteria that are not unique to its own identity. The HB does not offer much aid in this endeavor despite its strong desire to ascribe the status of "nation" to Israel at an early point.[34] Though scholars present an array of arguments regarding the exact time when Israel became a nation, most scholars tend to ignore the two features that define a nation: a governing law and the possession of land.

---

31. Frank, "Recrafting Israel," 325. See also Mullen Jr., *Narrative History*, 57.
32. Frank, "Recrafting Israel," 319.
33. Frank, "Recrafting Israel," 321.
34. Frank, "Recrafting Israel," 317.

## Law

Unfortunately, using the Mosaic law as a defining feature of "national Israel" is not without its challenges. One such challenge is the definition of the term *tôrāh*. On the surface, the term denotes teaching or instruction rather than a politically charged legal code:

> Specifically, law refers to any set of regulations; e.g., Exod 12 contains the law in regard to observing the Passover. Some other specific laws include those for the various offerings (Lev 7:37), for leprosy (Lev 14:57) and for jealousy (Num 5:29). In this light law is often considered to consist of statutes, ordinances, precepts, commandments, and testimonies. The meaning of the word gains further perspective in the light of Deuteronomy. According to Deut 1:5 Moses sets about to explain the law; law here would encompass the moral law, both in its apodictic and casuistic formulation, and the ceremonial law. The genius of Deuteronomy is that it interprets the external law in the light of its desired effect on man's inner attitudes. In addition, the book of Deuteronomy itself shows that the law has a broad meaning to encompass history, regulations and their interpretation, and exhortations. It is not merely the listing of casuistic statements as is the case in Hammurabi's code. Later the word extended to include the first five books of the Bible in all their variety.[35]

Deuteronomy 6:6–9 states that the Israelites were to teach the *tôrāh* to their children, which emphasizes its didactic purpose. On the other hand, the *tôrāh* also served as a legal code for the Israelites in religious and civic contexts.

Wellhausen popularized the "documentary hypothesis" in his *Prolegomena zur geschichte Israels*.[36] Given the resurgence of the

---

35. Hartley, "תּוֹרָה," *TWOT* 2:910.

36. The perspective of Wellhausen's hypothesis is regaining traction in mainstream scholarship. Baden summarizes, "The documentary hypothesis is intended to account for the penultimate stage of the text, the existence of the sources immediately before their combination into the canonical whole." Even so, he admits that "the Documentary Hypothesis must be recognized for what it is: a hypothesis." See Baden, *Composition of the Pentateuch*, 32.

documentary hypothesis in recent years, it is necessary to address the issue as it pertains to the *tôrāh* and national identity.[37] Wellhausen notes the legal requirements of the Pentateuch:

> The knowledge of God, which Hosea (chapter 4) regards as the contents of the Torah, has yet a closer connection with jurisprudence than with theology; but as its practical issue is that God requires of man righteousness, and faithfulness, and good-will, it is fundamentally and essentially morality, though morality at that time addressed its demands less to the conscience than to society. A ritual tradition naturally developed itself even before the exile (2 Kgs 17:27, 28). But only those rites were included in the Torah which the priests had to teach others, not those which they discharged themselves; even in Leviticus this distinction may be traced; the instructions characterized as toroth being chiefly those as to animals which might or might not be eaten, as to clean and unclean states, as to leprosy and its marks (cf. Deut 24:8). So it was in Israel, to which the testimony applies which we have cited: and so it was in Judah also.[38]

Wellhausen observes that the *tôrāh*, because it is from God, is essentially moral, and this morality concerns benevolent care, justice, and loyalty. As such, for Wellhausen, *tôrāh* is not in its entirety theological. Wellhausen ascribes the law as jurisprudence rather than religious dogma.[39] Following Wellhausen to some degree, David Carr suggests that the Pentateuch became legally binding during Josiah's reform.[40]

Both Wellhausen and Carr assume a redacted approach to the Pentateuch. While such approaches may lead to a discovery of the final composition of the Pentateuch, it does not address the now-actions of the final scene within the exodus narrative which attributes the authority of the *tôrāh* to the narrative of Deut 5:1.

---

37. For recent work on the documentary hypothesis, see Baden, *Composition of the Pentateuch*, 12.
38. Wellhausen, *Prolegomena*, 395–96.
39. Wellhausen, *Prolegomena*, 395.
40. Carr, "Rise of Torah," 47.

Helpfully, Childs championed the view that the final form of the text is the form that one should study. Childs does not promote his method as another critical approach to the text but argues that this approach serves as a hermeneutic for reading Scripture in which one looks for the canonical context and shape.[41]

From the narrator's perspective, the Israelites possessed a legally binding code prior to and required for their entry into Canaan. The giving of the law before Israel's entry into Canaan implies that they were no longer subject to other legal codes. The exodus and the subsequent journey to the promised land necessitated a legal framework. The *tôrāh* provided this framework, establishing the foundations of a nation by defining the people's relationship with Yahweh and with one another.

The legal provisions of the *tôrāh* structured Israel's governance and provided a framework for resolving disputes. This legal system promoted fairness and justice, enabling the stability of the nation. Furthermore, the *tôrāh* addressed the role of its leaders, stating that they too were subject to the legal constraints of the law. In this manner, the law developed a sense of collective purpose by committing to a shared set of values and beliefs.

## Land

The physical territory occupied by a nation plays a fundamental role in defining the identity of a nation. Goodblatt observes, "The concept of a nation can and should be distinguished from that of a state."[42] Land serves as the backdrop on which to write a nation's history, culture, and collective memory. Thus, the sum of ethnic and territorial parts tend to define a nation; however, this view makes national identity a fluid concept.

Land serves as the setting for collective memories and historical narratives. Within national borders, landmarks and

---

41. Childs introduces his approach in his *Introduction to the Old Testament as Scripture*. For an analysis of Childs's approach, see Kittel, "Brevard Childs's Development," 2–11; Brueggemann, "Brevard Childs's Canon Criticism," 312.

42. Goodblatt, *Elements of Ancient Jewish Nationalism*, 26.

monuments become tangible links to the past. Both natural and manufactured landmarks define national identity. The narratives of the exodus and conquest present both types of landmarks as memorials. For example, Mt. Sinai is a natural landmark while Josh 4:1–9 offers an example of a constructed landmark:

> When the entire nation was on the other side, the LORD told Joshua, "Select for yourselves twelve men from the people, one per tribe. Instruct them, 'Pick up twelve stones from the middle of the Jordan, from the very place where the priests stand firmly, and carry them over with you and put them in the place where you camp tonight.'" Joshua summoned the twelve men he had appointed from the Israelites, one per tribe. Joshua told them, "Go in front of the ark of the LORD your God to the middle of the Jordan. Each of you is to put a stone on his shoulder, according to the number of the Israelite tribes. The stones will be a reminder to you. When your children ask someday, 'Why are these stones important to you?' tell them how the water of the Jordan stopped flowing before the ark of the covenant of the LORD. When it crossed the Jordan, the water of the Jordan stopped flowing. These stones will be a lasting memorial for the Israelites." The Israelites did just as Joshua commanded. They picked up twelve stones, according to the number of the Israelite tribes, from the middle of the Jordan as the LORD had instructed Joshua. They carried them over with them to the camp and put them there. Joshua also set up twelve stones in the middle of the Jordan in the very place where the priests carrying the ark of the covenant stood. They remain there to this very day.

These stones served as a permanent memorial intended to prompt Israel's memory of the crossing of the Jordan through intergenerational teaching.[43] This story passes from generation to generation by means of the landmark's heritage rather than the psychological memory of the event. The memory lasts as long as the landmark exists.

---

43. Dozeman, *Joshua 1–12*, 292.

The demarcation of borders defines territorial integrity and places limitations on its governing power. Yahweh delineates the borders of the promised land to the new generation of Israelites upon their entry into Canaan:

> Then the LORD spoke to Moses: "Give these instructions to the Israelites, and tell them: 'When you enter Canaan, the land that has been assigned to you as an inheritance, the land of Canaan with its borders, your southern border will extend from the wilderness of Zin along the Edomite border, and your southern border will run eastward to the extremity of the Salt Sea, and then the border will turn from the south to the Scorpion Ascent, continue to Zin, and then its direction will be from the south to Kadesh Barnea. Then it will go to Hazar Addar and pass over to Azmon. There the border will turn from Azmon to the Stream of Egypt, and then its direction is to the sea. And for a western border you will have the Great Sea. This will be your western border. And this will be your northern border: From the Great Sea you will draw a line to Mount Hor; from Mount Hor you will draw a line to Lebo Hamath, and the direction of the border will be to Zedad. The border will continue to Ziphron, and its direction will be to Hazar Enan. This will be your northern border. For your eastern border you will draw a line from Hazar Enan to Shepham. The border will run down from Shepham to Riblah, on the east side of Ain, and the border will descend and reach the eastern side of the Sea of Kinnereth. Then the border will continue down the Jordan River and its direction will be to the Salt Sea. This will be your land by its borders that surround it" (Num 34:1–12).

Genesis 15:18–21 offers another account of the borders of the promised land:

> That day the LORD made a covenant with Abram: "To your descendants I give this land, from the river of Egypt to the great river, the Euphrates River—the land of the Kenites, Kenizzites, Kadmonites, Hittites, Perizzites, Rephaites, Amorites, Canaanites, Girgashites, and Jebusites."

While the borders of Gen 15:18–21 and the borders of Num 34:1–12 do not correspond entirely, Weinfeld notes that both are idealistic systems.[44] Wazana helpfully adds, "The differences in form and context reveal that these are two separate genres that convey two different conceptions of the promised land, but not two different territorial units."[45] However, Grosby questions the consensus that all borders in the ANE were unnuanced. He states, "Examination of evidence from the ancient Near East and Armenia, spanning a period of more than a thousand years, indicates the existence of conceptions of relatively precise boundaries, territories, and perhaps also nations."[46] Nations understood territorial limits. However, the degree to which these limits were concretely set cannot be known aside from the use of natural landmarks.

## Summary

Throughout the exodus, Yahweh takes a people with no formal law and no formal land to a setting in which both law and land both define and unify the group. The exodus is not merely a journey from one physical place to another but is a transitional period by which the Hebrews become "national Israel." Chapter 2 demonstrated in detail the degree to which the Israelites assimilated to Egyptian mores. Clearly, the Hebrews followed some form of a legal code while in Egypt. During the Late Bronze Age, Egyptian legal codes were deeply rooted in the concept of Maat—the principle of truth and balance in the cosmic order. This system reflected Egypt's focus on moral and social symmetry rather than a fixed legalistic framework.[47] Additionally, the Hebrews occupied

---

44. Weinfeld, *Promise of the Land*, 55.

45. Wazana, "From Dan to Beer-Sheba," 63–64.

46. Grosby, "Borders, Territory and Nationality," 1.

47. Manning observes, "The concept of 'law' and 'justice' are intimately associated with the proper behavior of kings and were embedded in every royal ritual. They were also a frequent theme in literary portrayals of the 'good king.' Ordinary people, too, were governed by the same concept. Proper behavior was expected in all relationships, within the family, between neighbors, between officials and the governed, and so on." Manning, "Representation of

land (i.e., Goshen) while in Egyptian captivity, though they did not own or perhaps better stated possess the land they occupied. The giving of the law of Moses and the giving of the land of Canaan allowed the Israelites to possess what they did not uniquely have in Egypt.

## THE NEED TO RE-CIRCUMCISE IN JOSHUA 5:2-9

To this point, Josh 5:2–9 has served primarily as the catalyst for the present study. Here, we must dive into the pericope itself as its own now-action narrative. What information does the text give about its own narrative sequence?

Prior to their Egyptian captivity, the patriarchs and their tribe(s) were nomadic. They share similarities with their neighbors but retain their own cultural and religious mores (e.g., Gen 12:10–20; 14:1–24; 34:1–31). However, a cultural shift occurred during the Egyptian captivity in which the Israelites became culturally (and to some degree, religiously) Egyptian. At the end of the exodus, Yahweh gave the Israelites a law and land which ceased their nomadic nature and shaped their cultural distinctiveness. Admittedly, scholars have long recognized that much of the Mosaic law placed restrictions on Canaanite rituals.[48] To be sure, the law of

Justice," 112.

48. For example, one explanation of the command to not cook a young goat in its mother's milk (Exod 23:19) is that such was a practice of the Canaanites in the region. For more on the command of cooking a young goat in its mother's milk, see Carmichael, "On Separating Life and Death," 1–7; Milgrom, "You Shall Not Boil," 48–55; Ratner and Zuckerman, "In Rereading," 56–58; and Haran, "Seething a Kid," 23–35. "The older sources show, accordingly, that the conquest of Canaan by Israel was a process that extended over several centuries. The aborigines were not exterminated, but certain Hebrew clans forced their way into the land, and occupied the rural districts, while the walled cities remained, for the most part, hands of the Canaanites. For a long while there was hostility between the two races; but gradually this ceased, and a process of amalgamation began. Cities that could not be conquered were eventually united to Israel by treaties that gave them full political rights. Whole tribes that made peace and accepted the worship of Yahweh were incorporated into the nation and counted as 'sons of Israel.' In process of time, through conquest, treaty, or inter-marriage, Canaanites and Hebrews were fused into one people

Moses certainly prohibits the religious and some cultural practices of the Canaanites, namely in their pagan worship practices. However, if we view Israel in contrast to Egypt (i.e., anti-Egypt) rather than in contrast to Canaan (a society relatively unknown to this generation of Israelites), a different hermeneutic of the Mosaic law and of the promised land in necessary.

Dietary and clothing restrictions in the law of Moses depict an anti-Egyptian agenda. The following chart demonstrates the contrasting juxtaposition between Egyptian mores and exodus events/laws.[49]

| Egyptian Mores | Exodus Events/Laws |
|---|---|
| Polytheism | Monotheism (Exod 20:3; Deut 6:4) |
| The use of idols | No graven image of Yahweh (Exod 20:4–6) |
| Wearing mixed material garments | Prohibition of mixed material garments (Lev 19:19; Deut 22:11) |
| Cross-dressing | Prohibition of wearing clothing belonging to the other gender (Deut 22:5) |
| Tattoos | Prohibition against tattoos (Lev 19:28) |
| Staple diet of Nile fish (esp. catfish) | Prohibition against water animals that do not have fins and scales (Lev 11:9–12) |
| Adult circumcision | 8th-day circumcision (Lev 12:3) |

Table 2: A Comparison of Egyptian Mores and the Law of Moses

---

and dwelt in the same cities, as was the case, for instance, in Shechem in the days of Abimelech (Judg 9)." Paton, "Canaanite Influence," 208.

49. Several mummies have been found with basic tattoos made with carbon. Elizabeth Kerner notes, "In ancient times, tattooing was an altogether dangerous undertaking, as the risk of infection was high due to suboptimal cleanliness and a lack of knowledge of hygiene. The skin was either cut with a sharp instrument and the pigment then rubbed into the wound, or the pigment was brought under the skin by repeated pricking with a pointed object. There are no ancient written records telling us how it was done, but as the most ancient forms of tattooing known to us were carried out in these ways, we have to assume that this was also the case in earlier times." Kerner, "Ancient Practice of Tattooing," 38.

The above chart is not exhaustive but illustrates the point. This hermeneutic suggests that Israel's time in the wilderness was transformative rather than formative *ex nihilo*. Thus, the shedding of a former Egyptian identity proves crucial to the development of Israel as a sovereign nation.

Taking this approach, the Israelites shed their Egyptian mores in four primary stages. The first occurs in their craving for Egyptian food. Though their cravings clouded their memories of enslavement, Yahweh provided quail and manna (Exod 16:13–15). The provision of food unknown in Egypt removes the more of food as culturally identifying. The second occurs when Moses destroyed the gold taken in the Egyptian plunder (Exod 3:22; cf. Deut 15:13) that formed the golden calf and then used the remainder of the jewelry (*'adî*) to construct the tabernacle and its contents. In doing so, Moses destroyed the mores of cultural luxury and nationally defining symbols. The third is the giving of the law of Moses. Niehaus observes, "Pharaohs claimed that the sun god Ra, their father, commanded them to promulgate laws the god had in mind and in general to do what Ra was doing."[50] Instead, the law of Moses rejects an earthy king and places Yahweh as the true king in Israel (cf. 1 Sam 8:7–8). The fourth stage is the mass circumcision that occurred before the second generation entered the promised land. As previously explored in chapter 3, there is strong evidence suggesting that adult circumcision replaced infant circumcision as the norm in Israelite culture based on the circumcision practices of the Egyptians. The circumcision of Josh 5:2–9 is a re-circumcision narrative in which Abrahamic circumcision—an essential component of the Abrahamic covenant—replaces Egyptian circumcision.

The formation of Israelite identity in the Hexateuch follows a chiastic structure in which circumcision frames descendant narratives.

    A. The promise of land (Gen 15)

        B. The institution of Abrahamic circumcision (Gen 17)

            C. Israel's (i.e., Jacob's) descendants (Gen 30:1–24; 35:15)

---

50. Niehaus, *Ancient Near Eastern Themes*, 57.

D. Israel in Egypt

 CC. Israel's descendants of the second generation (Josh 5:4)

  BB. Circumcision of the second generation (Josh 5:2–9)

   AA. The obtaining of land (Josh 5:10–12)

Circumcision was not unique to Israel. In addition to the Egyptians, the Midianites and the Phoenicians also observed the rite.[51] Thus, Israel's practice of circumcision alone cannot forthrightly place them in terms of "otherness"—i.e., uniquely distinct from their neighbors. However, the theological basis on which Abrahamic circumcision rests places circumcision as a meaningful identifier for Israel's national identity. Deenick disagrees, arguing that different forms of circumcision (à la Sasson) do not appear in the text since it is the second generation that underwent circumcision rather than the generation of Egypt. However, Deenick's comment that "the text makes no room for a different kind of circumcision" ignores the historical now-actions of the exodus narrative.[52] If a previous Egyptian form of circumcision is synonymous with the "disgrace of Egypt" in Josh 5:9, as Sasson suggests and as this study has shown, there must be a theological issue with the Egyptianized form that does not uphold the dogmatic implications of circumcision for Israel.

Sasson helpfully notes the purpose of Egyptian circumcision:

> In Egypt, however, texts, sculptures, and mummies seem to support the conclusion that babies never underwent the operation; it was reserved for either a period of prenuptial ceremonies or, more likely, for initiation into the state of manhood. Still remaining to be decided is the question of whether circumcision among the Egyptians was voluntary or universally imposed; whether it was adopted by the common populace or reserved for a high

---

51. Scholars continue to debate the cultural and religious significance of circumcision. It seems doubtful that a consensus will occur. For a current bibliography on the issue, see Isaac, "Circumcision," 444–56.

52. Deenick, *Righteous by Promise*, 68.

caste which included the pharaoh, his priests, his courtiers, and his immediate servants.[53]

Abrahamic circumcision differs from Egyptian circumcision in occasion, method, and meaning.[54] The occasion of Abrahamic circumcision is the eighth day of a male child's life. Circumcision never appears in the HB as a rite representing entrance into adulthood or as a prerequisite for prenuptial events. Maimonides (1138–1204), a Sephardic rabbi and philosopher, offers three reasons in favor of infant circumcision:

> The first is that were the child let alone until he grew up, he would sometimes not perform it. The second is that a child does not suffer as much pain as a grown-up man because his membrane is still soft and his imagination is weak; for a grown-up man would regard the thing, which he would imagine before it occurred, as terrible and hard. The third is that the parents of a child that is just born take lightly matters concerning it, for up to that time the imaginative form that compels the parents to love it is not yet consolidated.... Consequently, if it were left uncircumcised for two or three years, this would necessitate the abandonment of circumcision because of the father's love and affection for it. At the time of its birth, on the other hand, this imaginative form is very weak, especially as far as concerns the father upon whom this commandment is imposed.[55]

The method of circumcision in Josh 5:2–9 heavily contrasts with the precise surgical technique of adult circumcision in Egypt in which surgeons, assistants, and metal tools were used. On the other hand, the re-circumcision of Josh 5:2–9 used flint knives, which, as Sasson suggests, calls the mind back to the archaic historical

---

53. Sasson, "Circumcision," 474.

54. The rabbis submitted to the act of *peri'ah* ("opening" or "uncovering"). This was the act of removing the entire foreskin. If a shred of the foreskin remained, the circumcision was invalid. Glick, *Marked in Your Flesh*, 45.

55. Maimonides, *Guide of the Perplexed*, 609.

beginning of Abrahamic circumcision.[56] Egyptian circumcision denoted maturity, authority, and divinity in some cases:

> A passage from the Book of the Dead speaks of the god Re's self-induced circumcision. The king of Egypt, as the son and the representation of this divinity, probably underwent the same operation as he entered manhood. This possibly self-imposed immolation may find a parallel in the experience of Abraham (Gen 17) and that of Bata in the Egyptian tale of the Two Brothers. Sesostris I is known have remarked: "As a child, when I had not yet lost my foreskin . . ." (Stracman, *AIEP*, 8–9). Similarly, Khnumhotpe, monarch of Beni-Hassan during the XII Dynasty, boasted that his father "governed at a time when he had not yet lost prepuce" (Urk. 7:34). The rite appears thus to have been unconnected with accession to power, at least in Egypt.[57]

Abrahamic circumcision offered no implications for the establishment of authority or divinity. Circumcision in Israel was never based on class or social function.

Rupert of Deutz, an influential Benedictine theologian in the twelfth century, likened Abraham's circumcision to his faith, stating, "Thus rightly, in the same way for Abraham, because he believed God saying that in his seed all nation would be blessed, in the place of the seed, that is, in the genital part of the body, a sign of that same faith was placed."[58] Circumcision served as a reminder that Yahweh would fulfill the promise through Abraham's seed (*zera'*). As such, Josh 5:2–9 is disconnected from the conquest narratives that ensue shortly thereafter. Circumcision was not merely a physical act but a symbol of commitment to God's covenant promises, a sign of separation from other nations, and a means of ensuring continuity of the covenant lineage. The circumcision of the second-generation Israelite males in Josh 5:2–9 presents the renewal of the Abrahamic covenant with God. The

---

56. Sasson, "Circumcision," 475.
57. Sasson, "Circumcision," 474.
58. Deenick, *Righteous by Promise*, 49.

act emphasizes Israel's dependence on divine favor and protection as they embark on the conquest. It symbolizes their obedience to God's commandments by emphasizing that their success is contingent on their faithfulness to the Abrahamic covenant, which the conquest would fulfill. In this light, the re-circumcision narrative expresses deep theological significance.

## CONCLUSION

The re-circumcision narrative in Josh 5:2–9 serves as a theological and covenantal fulcrum in Israel's transition from an Egyptian-influenced nomadic group to a distinct nation under Yahweh's sovereignty. By reinstating the Abrahamic practice of circumcision, the Israelites symbolically shed remnants of Egyptian cultural assimilation and reaffirm their covenant promise of land and descendants. This act encapsulates the theological separation from Egypt, the physical reestablishment of covenantal identity, and the communal readiness to possess the promised land. Through this lens, the re-circumcision event becomes more than an isolated ritual. It is a pivotal moment of consecration that defines Israel's emergent nationhood.

# 6

# Conclusion

THE EXODUS NARRATIVE PRESENTS a series of mysteries in what it says and more intriguingly what it leaves unsaid. Issues of the exodus's date, the identity of the Pharaoh, and the chronology of its events continue to plague scholars. The study undertaken in this book addresses the intersection of theology, cultural anthropology, and literary criticism by examining circumcision within the historical, religious, and social frameworks of ancient Israel's formation.

At its core, this study interrogates the neglect and eventual re-implementation of circumcision during the wilderness periods. This analysis foregrounds three significant conclusions. First, circumcision functioned as a marker of covenantal loyalty, reclaiming its identity from the Egyptian cultural milieu. Through comparative analyses of Egyptian circumcision practices, this study demonstrated that the re-circumcision narrative of Josh 5:2–9 embodied a theological separation from Egyptian religious norms.

Second, the study critiqued Moses's relationship with circumcision. Moses's narrative is characterized by tension between his Egyptian identity and his role as the divinely appointed leader of Israel. The "bridegroom of blood" episode (Exod 4:24–26) serves as a pivotal moment in the text, where Moses's neglect of circumcision is corrected through Zipporah's action. Moses's internal

CONCLUSION

conflict deepens his narrative characterization and clarifies the broader theme of Israel's struggle to fully embrace its covenantal obligations.

Third, the re-circumcision of Israel's second generation under Joshua marks a climactic moment in the narrative, symbolizing the nation's willingness to inherit the promised land. This act is more than a ritualistic renewal; it is a redemptive reclamation of Israel's identity as Yahweh's chosen people. The act's timing (immediately preceding the conquest of Canaan) underscores its theological and narrative significance. By "removing the disgrace of Egypt," Joshua's leadership solidifies the metamorphosis of the group of former slaves into a unified nation under divine governance.

## RECOMMENDATIONS FOR FURTHER RESEARCH

Scholarship has made great strides in the past fifty years concerning the historical facts of the exodus; however, few have taken up the mantle to combine these facts with the literary narrative of the text. *The Art of Biblical Narrative* by Robert Alter has served as the guidebook for narrative criticism over the past thirty years. However, Alter freely admits the shortcomings of narrative criticism:

> In recent years, there has been growing interest in literary approaches among the younger generation of Bible scholars . . . but, while useful explications of particular texts have begun to appear, there have been as yet no major works of criticism, and certainly no satisfying overviews of the poetics of the Hebrew Bible.[1]

Alter's call for further research bleeds into the plea here. There is a need for scholars to blend methods of critical interpretation that remain fair to both approaches. Historical critics tend to use the text as a supplement to archaeological data while literary critics tend to focus on syntactical structure alone, ignoring the historical evidence that frames the text. To that end, the use of the "now-actions" perspective deserves further critique and exploration. The

---

1. Alter, *Art of Biblical Narrative*, 16.

now-actions of a narrative allow the reader to evaluate details that are in the text based on those things that are not obviously stated in the text. Scholars must reframe their approaches to the biblical text in a way that emphasizes the whole.

On the historical-critical front, further research is needed concerning the practices of circumcision in the ANE and during the Egyptian middle and new kingdoms. The work of Sasson and Blaschke have proven indispensable in this process. Although Sasson explores evidence for circumcision in the ANE, he does not offer concrete reasons why various cultures separate from the Hebrews practiced the rite. More work is needed concerning circumcision's role as a marriage, maturity, and divinity rite. If one takes the position that Israel adopted an Egyptian form of circumcision as their practice, the theological implications of this custom may be more significant than previously thought.

Finally, while scholars such as Deenick have explored the theological implications of circumcision, further research is necessary regarding instances in which circumcision does not occur where one might expect to find it. This observation prompted the present study and has prompted a future study currently underway concerning the absence of circumcision in the NT book of Hebrews. Such a study must evaluate the identity of the *spermatos Abraam* in Heb 2:16 and the significance of faith as an identifying mark for the people of God throughout the book. In this sense, faith can be understood as the new circumcision which identifies the believer as a part of God's people. A full exploration of faith and circumcision in the NT is essential for developing a full biblical and systematic theology of identity.

## CONCLUSION

This study employed a methodology that combines historical-cultural and narrative-critical readings of the exodus narrative to address the need for a re-circumcision of Israelite men in Josh 5:2–9. By doing so, this study demonstrated that Israel's assimilation to Egyptian cultural and religious mores was greater than generally

## CONCLUSION

thought. By applying historical and literary critical approaches to the exodus narrative, this study established that the mores of Egypt impacted the mores of Israel extending throughout the exodus narrative and ceasing with the re-circumcision narrative of Josh 5:2–9. The need to circumcise "again" (*šēnît*; Josh 5:2) revealed that practice was neglected during the exodus; however, the text does not forthrightly state the reason. Based on the evidence presented in chapters 2 and 3, this study suggested two primary reasons for the neglect of Abrahamic circumcision: (1) an assimilation to Egyptian circumcision and (2) the lack of leadership displayed by the literary characterization of Moses. To become "national Israel," these mores must shed. The need to re-circumcise reflected the final stage of becoming a group that is anti-Egypt, its own nation, and the proper recipients of the Abrahamic promises.

# Bibliography

Ackroyd, Peter. *Exile and Restoration: A Study of Hebrew Thought of the Sixth Century B.C.* Philadelphia: Westminster, 1968.

Aichele, George, et al. "An Elephant in the Room: Historical-Critical and Postmodern Interpretations of the Bible." *JBL* 128 (2009) 383–404.

Ahlström, Gösta W. *Who Were the Israelites?* Winona Lake, IN: Eisenbrauns, 1986.

Allen, James. *Middle Egyptian: An Introduction to the Language and Culture of Hieroglyphs.* Cambridge: Cambridge University Press, 2014.

Allison, Dale. *The New Moses: A Matthean Typology.* Eugene, OR: Wipf & Stock, 1993.

Alter, Robert. *The Art of Biblical Narrative.* New York: Basic, 2011.

Assmann, Jan. *Moses the Egyptian: The Memory of Egypt in Western Monotheism.* Cambridge, MA: Harvard University Press, 1997.

———. *Of God and Gods: Egypt, Israel, and the Rise of Monotheism.* Madison: University of Wisconsin Press, 2008.

Auerbach, Eric. *Mimesis: The Representation of Reality in Western Literature.* Translated by Willard R. Trask. 50th ann. ed. Princeton: Princeton University Press, 2003.

Badawy Alexander. *The Tomb of Nyhetep-Ptah at Giza and the Tomb of Ankhmahor at Saqqara.* Berkeley: University of California Press, 1978.

Baden, Joel. *The Composition of the Pentateuch: Renewing the Documentary Hypothesis.* New Haven: Yale University Press, 2012.

Bailey, Randall. *Exodus.* The College Press NIV Commentary. Joplin, MO: College, 2007.

Bakan, David. *Sigmund Freud and the Jewish Mystical Tradition.* Mineola, NY: Dover, 2004.

Bakon, Shimon. "Jacob: The Father of a Nation." *JBQ* 28 (2000) 38–44.

Barr, James. "Child's Introduction to the Old Testament as Scripture." *JSOT* 16 (1980) 12–23.

Bartholomew, Craig. *The Old Testament and God: Old Testament Origins and the Question of God.* Grand Rapids: Baker Academic, 2022.

# BIBLIOGRAPHY

Barton, John. "Law and Narrative in the Pentateuch." *Communio Viatorum* 51 (2009) 126–40.

———. *Reading the Old Testament*. Philadelphia: Westminster, 1984.

Bayles, Lewis Paton. "Canaanite Influence on the Religion of Israel." *AJT* 18 (1914) 205–24.

Beal, Jane, ed. *Illuminating Moses: A History of Reception from Exodus to the Renaissance*. Vol. 4 of *Commentaria: Sacred Texts and Their Commentaries: Jewish, Christian, and Islamic*. Boston: Brill, 2014.

Bernat, David A. *Sign of the Covenant: Circumcision in the Priestly Tradition*. Atlanta: Society of Biblical Literature, 2009.

Blaschke, Andreas. *Beschneidung: Zeugnisse der Bibel und verwandter Texte*. Tübingen: Francke Verlag, 1998.

Bloch-Smith, Elizabeth. "Israelite Ethnicity in Iron I: Archaeology Preserves What Is Remembered and What is Forgotten in Israel's History." *JBL* 122 (2003) 401–25.

Bloom, Harold. "From J to K, or the Uncanniness of the Yahwist." In *The Bible and the Narrative Tradition*, edited by Frank McConnell. New York: Oxford University Press, 1986.

Boice, James. *Joshua: An Expositional Commentary*. Grand Rapids: Baker, 1989.

Borgen, Peder. *Philo of Alexandria: An Exegete for His Time*. Leiden: Brill, 1997.

Brier, Bob, and Hoyt Hobbs. *Daily Life of the Ancient Egyptians*. Westport, CT: Greenwood, 2008.

Brown, Raymond. *The Birth of the Messiah*. Garden City, NY: Doubleday, 1977.

Brueggemann, Dale. "Brevard Child's Canonical Criticism: An Example of Post-Critical Naiveté." *JETS* 32 (1989) 311–26.

Bulmer, Ralph. "The Uncleanness of the Birds of Leviticus and Deuteronomy." *Man* 24 (1989) 304–21.

Burrell, Kevin. *Cushites in the Hebrew Bible: Negotiating Ethnic Identity in the Past and Present*. Leiden: Brill, 2020.

Butler, Trent. "An Anti-Moses Tradition." *JSOT* 12 (1979) 9–15.

———. *Joshua*. Word Biblical Commentary 7. Waco, TX: Word, 1983.

Camp, Claudia. *Wise, Strange and Holy*. JSOTSS 320. Sheffield: Sheffield Academic Press, 2000.

Carmichael, Calum. "On Separating Life and Death: An Explanation of Some Biblical Laws." *HTR* 69 (1976) 1–7.

Carr, David. "The Rise of Torah." In *The Pentateuch as Torah: New Models for Understanding Its Promulgation and Acceptance*. Edited by Gary Koppers and Bernard Levinson. Winona Lake, IN: Eisenbrauns, 2007.

Cassuto, Umberto. *A Commentary on the Book of Exodus*. Jerusalem: Magnes, 1997.

Charles, R. H. *The Book of Jubilees or the Little Genesis*. London: Adam and Clark Black, 1902.

Chazan, Michael, and Mark Lehner. "An Ancient Analogy: Pot Baked Bread in Ancient Mesopotamia and Egypt." *Paléorient* 16 (1990) 21–35.

# BIBLIOGRAPHY

Clutton-Brock, Juliet. *Animals as Domesticates: A World View Through History.* East Lansing, MI: Michigan State University Press, 2012.

Coats, George. "Despoiling the Egyptians." *VT* 18 (1968) 450–57.

———. *Moses: Heroic Man, Man of God.* JSOTSS 57. Sheffield: Sheffield Academic, 1988.

———. "Moses in Midian. *JBL* 92 (1973) 3–10.

Cohen, Shaye J. D. *The Beginnings of Jewishness: Boundaries, Varieties, and Uncertainties.* Los Angeles: University of California Press, 1999.

Collins, N. C. "Evidence in the Septuagint of a Tradition in which the Israelites Left Egypt without Pharaoh's Consent." *CBQ* 56 (1994) 442–48.

Coogan, Michael David, and Mark S. Smith, eds. *Stories from Ancient Canaan.* Louisville: Westminster John Knox Press, 2012.

Creach, Jerome. *Joshua.* IBC. Louisville: Westminster John Knox, 2003.

Currid, John. *Ancient Egypt and the Old Testament.* Grand Rapids: Baker Academic, 1997.

Dalman, Rodger. "Egypt and Early Israel's Cultural Setting: A Quest for Evidential Possibilities." *JETS* 51 (2008) 449–88.

D'Amico, Davide. "What Is Not, But Might Be: Disnarration as Narrative in the Hebrew Bible." *JETS* 142 (2023) 183–96.

Damgaard, Fin. "Philo's Life of Moses as 'Rewritten Bible.'" In *Rewritten Bible After Fifty Years: Texts, Terms, or Techniques?* Edited by József Zsengellér. Leiden: Brill, 2014.

David, Rosalie. *The Ancient Egyptians: Religious Beliefs and Practices.* London: Routledge, 1982.

Davies, Gordon F. *Israel in Egypt: Reading Exodus 1–2.* Journal for the Study of the Old Testament Supplement Series. Sheffield: Sheffield Academic Press, 1992.

Deenick, Karl. *Righteous by Promise: A Biblical Theology of Circumcision.* Grand Rapids: InterVarsity, 2018.

Delitzsch, Franz. *New Commentary on Genesis.* Translated by Sophia Taylor. 2 vols. New York: Scribner & Welford, 1889.

Dever, William. *Who Were the Early Israelites and Where Did They Come From?* Grand Rapids: Eerdmans, 2003.

Diamond, Kelly-Anne. "Hatshepsut: Transcending Gender in Ancient Egypt." *Gender & History* 32 (2020) 168–88.

Dick, Michael. *Born in Heaven, Made on Earth: The Making of Cult Images in the Ancient Near East.* Winona Lake, IN: Eisenbrauns, 1999.

Dobanovacki, Dusanka, et al. "Surgery Before Common Era (B.C.E.)." *Archive of Oncology* 20 (2012) 28–35.

Donaldson, Terence. *Judaism and the Gentiles: Jewish Patterns of Universalism to 135 CE.* Waco, TX: Baylor University Press, 2007.

Drower, Margaret. *Flinders Petrie: A Life in Archaeology.* Wisconsin Studies in Classics. Madison, WI: University of Wisconsin Press, 1995.

Dozeman, Thomas. *Exodus.* Grand Rapids: Eerdmans, 2009.

———. *Joshua 1-12: A New Translation with Introduction and Commentary.* New Haven: Yale University Press, 2015.

———. "Masking Moses and Mosaic Authority in Torah." *JBL* 119 (2000) 21-45.

———. Thomas Römer, and Konrad Schmid. *Pentateuch, Hexateuch, or Enneateuch?: Identifying Literary Works in Genesis through Kings.* Atlanta: Society of Biblical Literature, 2011.

Dumbrell, W. "Exodus 4:24-25: A Textual Re-examination." *HTR* 65 (1972) 285-90.

Durham, John I. *Exodus.* WBC 3. Grand Rapids: Zondervan, 2015.

Eakin, Frank Jr. "Yahwism and Baalism Before the Exile." *JBL* 84 (1965) 407-14.

Eilberg-Schwartz, Howard. *God's Phallus: And Other Problems for Men and Monotheism.* Boston: Beacon, 1994.

El-Gawhary, Karim. "Religious Ferment(ation)." *MERIP* 211 (1999) 14-15.

Ellingworth, Paul. *The Epistle to the Hebrews.* Grand Rapids: Eerdmans, 1993.

Embry, Bradley. "The Endangerment of Moses: Towards a New Reading of Exodus 4:24-26." *VT* 2010 (60) 177-96.

Enns, Peter. *Exodus.* Grand Rapids: Zondervan, 2000.

Estelle, Bryan D. *Echoes of Exodus: Tracing a Biblical Motif.* Downers Grove, IL: IVP Academic, 2018.

Epstein, Isidore, ed. *The Hebrew-English Edition of the Babylonian Talmud.* 30 vols. London: Soncino, 1965-89.

Eusebius. *The Preparation for the Gospel.* Translated by Edwin Hamilton Gifford. Oxford: Clarendon, 1903.

Eyre, Stephen. *Moses: Calling and Character.* Downers Grove, IL: InterVarsity Press, 2011.

Farber, Zev. *Images of Joshua in the Bible and Their Reception.* Berlin: De Gruyter, 2016.

Farisani, Elelwani. "A Sociological Analysis of Israelites in Babylonian Exile." *OTE* 17 (2004) 380-88.

Feldman, Louis. "Josephus's Portrait of Moses." *JQR* 82 (1992) 285-328.

———. "Moses in Midian, According to Philo." *Shofar* 21 (2003) 1-20.

———. *Philo's Portrayal of Moses in the Context of Ancient Judaism.* Notre Dame, IN: University of Notre Dame Press, 2007.

———. "Philo's View of Moses' Birth and Upbringing." *CBQ* 64 (2002) 253-81.

Fontinoy, C. "Les noms de lieux en *-ayim* dans la Bible." *UF* 3 (1971) 33-40.

Fox, Nili Sacher, et al., eds. *The Body: Lived, Cultured, Adorned: Essays on Dress and the Body in the Bible and Ancient Near East in Honor of Nili S. Fox.* Cincinnati: Hebrew Union College Press, 2022.

Frank, Nathan Dwight. "Recrafting Israel: Toward an Ethnotechnical Conception of the Nation." *BibInt* 23 (2015) 316-39.

Frazer, James George. *The Golden Bough: A Study in Magic and Religion.* London: Oxford University Press, 1994.

Friedlander, Gerald, ed. *Pirkê de Rabbi Eliezer.* New York: Kegan Paul, Trench, Trubner & Co., 1916.

# BIBLIOGRAPHY

Friedman, Ira. "And Upon all the Gods of Egypt I Will Execute Judgment: The Egyptian Deity in the Ten Plagues." *Trad* 48 (2015) 8–18.

Friedman, Richard. *The Exodus: How it Happened and Why it Matters*. New York: HarperOne, 2017.

Gadeloff, David. "How Long Was the Sojourn in Egypt: 210 or 430 Years?" *JBQ* 44 (2016) 183–89.

Gardiner, Alan. "The Egyptian Origin of Some English Personal Names." *JAOS* 56 (1936) 189–97.

Gesenius, Friedrich Heinrich Wilhelm. *Gesenius' Hebrew Grammar*. Oxford: Clarendon, 1910.

Glick, Leonard B. *Marked in Your Flesh: Circumcision from Ancient Judea to Modern America*. Oxford: Oxford University Press, 2005.

Goodblatt, David. *Elements of Ancient Jewish Nationalism*. New York: Cambridge University Press, 2006.

Goodnick, Benjamin. "Israel's Defining Experience: From Family to Nation." *JBQ* 27 (1999) 192–94.

Gorospe, Arthena. *Narrative and Identity: An Ethical Reading of Exodus 4*. Leiden: Brill, 2007.

Goswell, Greg. "The Non-Royal Portrayal of Moses in the Pentateuch." *JESOT* 7 (2021) 60–81.

Grässer, Erich. *Der Glaube im Hebräerbrief*. Marburg: Elwert, 1965.

Gregory. *De Vita Moysis*. Translated by Herbertus Musurillo. Leiden: Brill, 1991.

———. *The Life of Moses*. Edited by Abraham J. Malherbe. The Classics of Western Spirituality. New York: Paulist, 1978.

Grosby, Steven. "Borders, Territory and Nationality in the Ancient Near East and Armenia." *Journal of the Economic and Social History of the Orient* 40 (1997) 1–29.

Hall, Christopher. "Moses and the Church Fathers." In *Illuminating Moses: A History of Reception from Exodus to the Renaissance*. Edited by Jane Beal. Leiden: Brill, 2014.

Hallo, William W. "The Concept of Canonicity in Cuneiform and Biblical Literature: A Comparative Appraisal." In *The Biblical Canon in Comparative Perspective: Scripture in Context IV*, edited by K. Lawson Younger Jr., et al., 1–19. Lewiston, NY: Mellen, 1991.

Halpern, Baruch. *The Emergence of Israel in Canaan*. Chico, CA: Scholars, 1983.

Hamilton, Victor P. *Exodus: An Exegetical Commentary*. Grand Rapids: Baker Academic, 2011.

———. *The Book of Genesis: Chapters 1–17*. NICOT. Grand Rapids: Eerdmans, 1990.

Haran, M. "Seething a Kid in Its Mother's Milk." *JJS* 30 (1979) 23–35.

Harris, R. Laird, et al., eds. *Theological Wordbook of the Old Testament*. 2 vols. Chicago: Moody, 1980.

# BIBLIOGRAPHY

Hartmann, Von Thomas A. G. "Mose und Maria 'Amuns Kind und Liebling': Auf den ägyptisehen Spuren zweier biblischer Namen." *ZAW* 116 (2004) 616–22.

Hasty, Jennifer, et al. *Introduction to Anthropology*. Houston, TX: OpenStax, 2022.

Hess, Richard. *Israelite Religion: An Archaeological and Biblical Survey*. Grand Rapids: Baker Academic, 2007.

Heiser, Michael. *Angels: What the Bible Really Says about God's Heavenly Hosts*. Bellingham, WA: Lexham, 2018.

———. "Deuteronomy 32:8 and the Sons of God." *BSac* 158 (2001) 52–74.

———. "Does Deuteronomy 32:17 Assume or Deny the Reality of Other Gods?" *BT* 59 (2008) 137–45.

Helfgot, Nathaniel. "And Moses Struck the Rock: Numbers 20 and the Leadership of Moses." *Tradition* 27 (1993) 51–58.

Hendel, Ronald. "Israel Among the Nations: Biblical Culture in the Ancient Near East." In *Remembering Abraham: Culture, Memory, and History in the Hebrew Bible*, edited by Ronald Hendel, 3–30. Oxford: Oxford University Press, 2005.

Henze, Matthias, ed. *A Companion to Biblical Interpretation in Early Judaism*. Grand Rapids: Eerdmans, 2012.

Herodotus. *The Persian Wars*. Translated by A. D. Godley. LCL. Cambridge, MA: Harvard University Press, 1920.

Hoenig, Sidney. "Circumcision: The Covenant of Abraham." *JQR* 53 (1963) 322–34.

Hoffmeier, James. *Ancient Israel in Sinai: The Evidence for the Authenticity of the Wilderness Tradition*. New York: Oxford University Press, 2005.

———. "Egyptian Religious Influences on the Early Hebrews." In *"Did I Not Bring Israel Out of Egypt?": Biblical, Archaeological, and Egyptological Perspectives on the Exodus Narratives*, edited by James Hoffmeier et al., 3–36. Winona Lake, IN: Eisenbrauns, 2016.

———. *Israel in Egypt*. New York: Oxford University Press, 1996.

Homan, Michael. "A Tensile Etymology for Aaron." *BN* 95 (1998) 21–22.

Houtman, Cornelis. *Exodus*. Translated by Sierd Woudstra. 3 vols. Leuven: Peters, 2000.

Huffmon, H. B. "Name." In *Dictionary of Deities and Demons in the Bible*, edited by Bob Becking Karel van der Toorn and Pieter W. van der Horst, 610–12. Grand Rapids: Eerdmans, 1999.

Hurvitz, Avi. "The Usage of Šēš and Bûṣin the Bible and Its Implication for the Date of P." *HTR* 60 (1967) 117–21.

Isaac, Erich. "Circumcision as a Covenant Rite." *Anthropos* 1964 (59) 444–56.

Jacobson, Rolf. "Moses, the Golden Calf, and the False Images of the True God." *WW* 33 (2013) 130–39.

Jenson, Robert. "Gregory of Nyssa: The Life of Moses." *ThTo* 62 (2006) 533–37.

Josephus. *Josephus*. Translated by Henry St. J. Thackeray et al. 10 vols. LCL. Cambridge: Harvard University Press, 1926–65.

# Bibliography

Kadari, Tamar. "Jochebed: Midrash and Aggadah." *Jewish Women: A Comprehensive Historical Encyclopedia*. Jewish Women's Archive, December 31, 1999. https://jwa.org/encyclopedia/article/jochebed-midrash-and-aggadah.

Kanarek, Jane L. *Biblical Narrative and the Formation of Rabbinic Law*. New York: Cambridge University Press, 2014.

Kaplan, Lawrence. "And the LORD Sought to Kill Him." *HAR* 5 (1981) 65–74.

Kass, Leon. *Founding God's Nation: Reading Exodus*. New Haven, CT: Yale University Press, 2021.

Kidner, Derek. *Jeremiah*. Downers Grove, IL: InterVarsity Press, 2014.

Kimball, Bruce. "The Origin of the Sabbath and Its Legacy to the Modern Sabbatical." *JHE* 49 (1978) 303–15.

Kittel, Gerhard, and Gerhard Friedrich, eds. *Theological Dictionary of the New Testament*. Translated by Geoffrey W. Bromiley. 10 vols. Grand Rapids: Eerdmans, 1964–76.

Kittell, Bonnie. "Brevard Childs's Development of the Canonical Approach." *JSOT* 16 (1980) 2–11.

Kerner, Elisabeth. "The Ancient Practice of Tattooing." *Ancient Egypt Magazine* 13 (2012) 38–42.

Knoppers, Gary N. and Bernard M. Levinson, eds. *The Pentateuch As Torah: New Models for Understanding Its Promulgation and Acceptance*. Winona Lake, IN: Eisenbrauns, 2007.

Koehler, Ludwig, et al. *The Hebrew and Aramaic Lexicon of the Old Testament*. Translated and edited by Mervyn E. J. Richardson. 2 vols. Leiden: Brill, 2001.

Krause, Joachim. "Das Buch Josua Auf Griechisch: Jos 5:2–9 Als Ausnahme, Die Regel Bestätigt." *JNSL* 38 (2012) 23–58.

Lambdin, Thomas. "Egyptian Loan Words in the Old Testament." *JAOS* 73 (1953) 145–55.

Langner, Allan. "The Golden Calf and Ra." *JBQ* 31 (2003) 43–47.

Leek, F. Filce. "Further Studies concerning Ancient Egyptian Bread." *JEA* 59 (1973) 199–204.

Leithart, Peter. "The Theology of the Drink Offering." *Theopolis*, July 17, 2018. https://theopolisinstitute.com/the-theology-of-the-drink-offering-2/.

Lesley, J. P. "Notes on an Egyptian Element in the Names of Hebrew Kings, and Its Bearing on the History of the Exodus." *PAPS* 108 (1881) 409–18.

Lévy, Carlos. "Philo of Alexandria." *The Stanford Encyclopedia of Philosophy*, February 5, 2018. Revised August 16, 2022. Edited by Edward N. Zalta and Uri Nodelman. https://plato.stanford.edu/archives/fall2022/entries/philo.

Lierman, John. *The New Testament Moses*. Tübingen: Mohr Siebeck, 2004.

Loewenstamm, Samuel. "The Making and Destruction of the Golden Calf." *Biblica* 48 (1967) 480–90.

MacLaurin, Evan Colin Briarcliffe. "YHWH, the Origin of the Tetragrammaton." *VT* 12 (1962) 439–63.

# BIBLIOGRAPHY

Maimonides, Moses. *The Guide of the Perplexed.* Translated and edited by Shlomo Pines. Chicago: University of Chicago Press, 1963.

Maksoud, Salwa, et al. "Beer from the Early Dynasties (3500–3400 cal. B.C. of Upper Egypt, Detected by Archaeological Methods." *Veget Hist Archaeobot* 3 (1994) 219–24.

Maller, Allen S. "The Bridegroom of Blood." *JBQ* 21 (1993) 94–98.

Malone, Andrew. "Distinguishing the Angel of the Lord." *BBR* 21 (2011) 297–314.

Mandelbaum, Bernard, ed. *The Midrash on Exodus: Translated and Annotated.* Vol. 2. New York: Jewish Publication Society, 1987.

Manning, J. G. "The Representation of Justice in Ancient Egypt." *Yale JL&H* 24 (2012) 111–18.

Marshall, I. Howard. *Acts: An Introduction and Commentary.* Downers Grove, IL: IVP Academic, 1980.

McDermott, John. *Reading the Pentateuch: A Historical Introduction.* New York: Paulist, 2002.

Megahed, Mohamed, and Hana Vymazalová. "Ancient Egyptian Royal Circumcision from the Pyramid Complex of Djedkare." *Anthropologie* 49 (2011) 155–64.

Meyers, Carol. "Having Their Space and Eating There Too: Bread Production and Female Power in Ancient Israelite Households." *Nashim* 5763 (2002) 14–44.

Meyer, Eduard. *Geschichte des Altertums: die altesten geschichtlichen Volker und Kulturen bis zum sechszehnten Jahrhundert.* Berlin: J. G. Cotta, 1913.

Milgrom, Jacob. "You Shall Not Boil a Kid in Its Mother's Milk." *BRev* 1 (1985) 48–55.

Morenz, Siegfried. *Egyptian Religion.* Translated by Ann E. Keep. Ithaca, NY: Cornell University Press, 1973.

Moazami, Mahnaz. "Evil Animals in the Zoroastrian Religion." *HR* 44 (2005) 300–317.

Muchiki, Yoshiyuki. *Egyptian Proper Names and Loanwords in North-West Semitic.* Atlanta: Society of Biblical Literature, 1999.

Muhs, Brian. "Ancient Egyptian Cuisine." *News and Notes* 237 (2018) 12–16.

Mullen, E. Theodore. *Narrative History and Ethnic Boundaries: The Deuteronomistic Historian and the Creation of Israelite Identity.* Atlanta: Scholars, 1993.

"NET Notes." *Netbible.org*, n.d. http://www.netbible.org.

Niehaus, Jeffrey. *Ancient Near Eastern Themes in Biblical Theology.* Grand Rapids: Kregel, 2008.

Nigosian, S. A. "Moses as They Saw Him." *VT* 43 (1993) 339–50.

Noth, Martin. *Die Israelitischen Personennamen im Rahmen der geminsemitischen Namengebung.* Hildesheim: Georg Olms, 1928.

———. *Exodus: A Commentary.* Translated by J. S. Bowden. Old Testament Library. Philadelphia: Westminster, 1962.

# Bibliography

O'Connell, Patrick F. "The Double Journey in Saint Gregory of Nyssa: The Life of Moses." *GOTR* 28 (1983) 301–24.

Origen. *On First Principles.* Translated by John C. Cavadini and Henri de Lubac. Notre Dame, IN: Christian Classics, 2013.

Paton, Lewis Bayles. "Canaanite Influence on the Religion of Israel." *AJT* 18 (1914) 205–24.

Pedersen, Johannes. *Israel: Its Life and Culture.* Atlanta: Scholars, 1991.

Peters, J. P. "The Religion of Moses." *JBL* 20 (1901) 101–28.

Petrie, William Matthew Flinders. *Egyptian Tales Translated from The Papyri: First Series, IVth to XIIth Dynasty.* New York: Frederick A. Stokes, 1899.

———. *The Religion of Ancient Egypt.* London: Archibald Constable & Co, 1908.

Philo. *On the Life of Moses Book I.* Translated by F. H. Colson. LCL. Cambridge: Harvard University Press, 1935.

———. *The Special Laws.* Translated by F. H. Colson. Vols. 7–8 of *Philo.* LCL. Cambridge: Harvard University Press, 1939.

Pinch, Geraldine. *Handbook of Egyptian Mythology.* Santa Barbra, CA: ABC-CLIO, 2002.

Poo, Mu-Chou. *Wine and Wine Offering in the Religion of Ancient Egypt.* New York: Routledge, 1995.

Porter, Bertha, and Rosalind Moss. *The Theban Necropolis: Part 1, Private Tombs.* Vol. 1 of *Topographical Bibliography of Ancient Egyptian Hieroglyphic Texts, Statues, Reliefs, and Paintings.* Oxford: Griffith Institute, 1960.

Pritchard, James B., ed. *Ancient Near Eastern Texts Relating to the Old Testament.* 3rd ed. Princeton: Princeton University Press, 1969.

Pseudo-Philo. *The Biblical Antiquities of Philo.* Translated by M. R. James. Eugene, Oregon: Wipf & Stock, 2006.

Quirke, Stephen. *The Cult of Ra.* London: Thames & Hudson, 2001.

Ratner, Robert, and B. Zuckerman. "In Rereading the 'Kid in Milk' Inscriptions." *BRev* 1 (1985) 56–58.

Redford, Donald. "The Hyksos Invasion in History and Tradition." *Orientalia* 39 (1970) 1–51.

Reeves, Nicholas. *The Complete Tutankhamun.* London: Thames & Hudson, 1995.

Reis, Pamela Tamarkin. "The Bridegroom of Blood: A New Reading." *Judaism* 40 (1991) 324–31.

Ringgren, Helmer. *Word and Wisdom: Studies in the Hypostatization of Divine Qualities and Functions in the Ancient Near East.* Lund: H. Ohlssons, 1947.

Ritner, Robert Kriech. *The Mechanics of Ancient Egyptian Magical Practice.* Chicago: University of Chicago Press, 1993.

———. "The Legend of Isis and the Name of Re." In *The Context of Scripture,* edited by William W. Hallo, 33–34. New York: Brill, 1997.

Robins, Gay. "Cult Statues in Ancient Egypt." In *Cult Image and Divine Representation in the Ancient Near East,* edited by Neal H. Walls. ASOR Book Series 10. Boston: American Schools of Oriental Research, 2005.

# BIBLIOGRAPHY

Rogland, Max. "Abram's Persistent Faith: Hebrew Verb Semantics in Genesis 15:6." *WTJ* (2008) 239–44.

Ross, Allen, and John Oswalt. *Genesis-Exodus*. Cornerstone Biblical Commentary. Edited by Philip W. Comfort. Carol Stream, IL: Tyndale, 2009.

Rubin, Aaron. "Egyptian Loanwords." In *Encyclopedia of Hebrew Language and Linguistics*, edited by Geoffrey Khan. 4 vols. Leiden: Brill, 2013.

Sasson, Jack. "Circumcision in the Ancient Near East." *JBL* 85 (1966) 473–76.

Sauneron, Serge. *The Priests of Ancient Egypt*. Translated by David Lorton. Ithaca, NY: Cornell University Press, 2000.

Savelle, Charles. "Acts 15:21: Moses is Preached and Read in the Synagogues." *JETS* 65 (2022) 707–17.

Schachter, Ariela. "From 'Different' to 'Similar': An Experimental Approach to Understanding Assimilation." *ASR* 81 (2016) 981–1013.

Sharps, Donald. *Sacred Bull, Holy Cow: A Cultural Study of Civilization's Most Important Animal*. New York: Peter Lang, 2006.

Sherwood, Aaron. "The Mixed Multitude in Exodus 12:38: Glorification, Creation, and Yahweh's Plunder of Israel and the Nations." *HBT* 34 (2012) 139–54.

Sklar, Jay. *Leviticus: An Introduction and Commentary*. Tyndale Old Testament Commentaries. Downers Grove, IL: IVP Academic, 2014.

Sneed, Mark. *The Social World of the Sages*. Minneapolis: Fortress, 2015.

Solomon, Zachary. "The Oldest Circumcision in the World." *Jewish Telegraphic Agency*, September 3, 2021. https://www.jta.org/jewniverse/2016/the-oldest-circumcision-in-the-world.

Sommer, Benjamin. *The Bodies of God and the World of Ancient Israel*. Cambridge: Cambridge University Press, 2009.

Spurrell, George James. *Notes on the Text of the Book of Genesis*. 2nd ed. Eugene, OR: Wipf & Stock, 2005.

Stein, Michael Alan. "The Religion of the Israelites in Egypt." *JBQ* 27 (2013) 195–99.

Steiner, Richard. "Incomplete Circumcision in Egypt and Edom: Jeremiah (9:24–25) in Light of Josephus and Jonckheere." *JBL* 118 (1999) 497–505.

Steinmann, Andrew E. *Genesis: An Introduction and Commentary*. TOTC. Downers Grove, IL: InterVarsity Press, 2019.

Sterling, Gregory. "The Interpreter of Moses: Philo of Alexandria and the Biblical Text." In *A Companion to Biblical Interpretation in Early Judaism*, edited by Matthias Henze. Grand Rapids: Eerdmans, 2012.

Stiebing, William Jr., and Susan N. Helft. *Ancient Near Eastern History and Culture*. 3rd ed. New York: Routledge, 2018.

Stripling, S., et al. "'You Are Cursed by the God YHW': An Early Hebrew Inscription from Mt. Ebal." *Herit Sci* 11 (2023) 1–24.

Stuart, Douglas. *Exodus*. The New American Commentary. Nashville: Broadman & Holman, 2006.

# BIBLIOGRAPHY

Teeter, Emily. *Religion and Ritual in Ancient Egypt*. Cambridge: Cambridge University Press, 2011.

Thiessen, Matthew. *Contesting Conversion: Genealogy, Circumcision, and Identity in Ancient Judaism and Christianity*. New York: Oxford University Press, 2011.

Thompson, James. *Hebrews*. Grand Rapids: Baker Academic, 2008.

Thompson, Thomas L., and Dorothy Irvin. "Joseph and Moses Narratives: Historical Reconstructions of the Narratives." In *Israelite and Judaean History*, edited by John H. Hayes and J. Maxwell Miller, 149–212. Philadelphia: Westminster, 1977.

Trachtenberg, Joshua. *Jewish Magic and Superstition: A Study in Folk Religion*. New York: Meridian, 1961.

Twersky, Geula. "An Examination of Aaron's Role in the Sin of the Golden Calf." *JBQ* 47 (2019) 55–63.

Ulmer, Rivka. "The Egyptian Gods in Midrashic Texts." *HTR* 103 (2010) 181–204.

Van Seters, John. *In Search of History: Historiography in the Ancient World and the Origins of Biblical History*. Winona Lake, IN: Eisenbrauns, 1997.

———. *The Pentateuch: A Social-Science Commentary*. Sheffield: Sheffield Academic, 1999.

Vermès, Géza, and József Zsengellér, eds. *Rewritten Bible After Fifty Years: Texts, Terms, or Techniques?: A Last Dialogue with Geza Vermes*. Supplements to the Journal for the Study of Judaism 166. Leiden: Brill, 2014.

Vögtle, Anton. "Die matthäische Kindheitsgeschichte." In *L'Evangile selon Matthieu: Rédaction et Théologiei*, edited by M. Didier, 153–83. BETL 29. Gembloux: Leuven University, 1972.

Volokhine, Youri. "Ancient Egyptian Food Prohibitions." *ANE Today*, August 4, 2022. https://www.asor.org/anetoday/2022/08/ancient-egyptian-food-prohibitions/.

Wallis, E. A. *The Book of the Dead: The Chapters of Coming Forth by Day; The Egyptian Text According to the Theban Recension in Hieroglyphic Edited from Numerous Papyri, with a Translation, Vocabulary, Etc.* London: Kegan Paul, Trench, Trübner & Co, 1898.

Walton, John, and D. Brent Sandy. *The Lost World of Scripture: Ancient Literary Culture and Biblical Authority*. Downers Grove, IL: IVP Academic, 2013.

Wasserman, James, and Eva Von Dassow. *The Egyptian Book of the Dead: The Book of Going Forth by Day*. San Francisco: Chronicle, 2008.

Wazana, Nili. "From Dan to Beer-Sheba and from the Wilderness to the Sea: Literal and Literary Images of the Promised Land in the Bible." In *Experiences of Place*, edited by Mary N. MacDonald, 45–86. Cambridge, MA: Center for the Study of World Religions, 2003.

Weinfeld, Moshe. *The Promise of the Land: The Inheritance of Canaan by the Israelites*. Berkeley, CA: University of California Press, 1993.

Wellhausen, Julius. *Prolegomena zur geschichte Israels*. Berlin: Druck und verlag von G. Reimer, 1899.

# BIBLIOGRAPHY

Wenham, Gordon. *Genesis 1–15*. WBC 1. Grand Rapids: Zondervan, 2014.

Wertz, Julie. "Unraveling the (Production) Secrets of an Egyptian Textile." *Harvard Art Museums*, May 28, 2020. https://harvardartmuseums.org/article/unraveling-the-production-secrets-of-an-egyptian-textile.

Westwood, Ursala. "Prophecies and Princesses: Moses in Egypt and Ethiopia According to Josephus." *Akroterion* 67 (2022) 65–85.

Wilkinson, Richard. *The Complete Temples of Ancient Egypt*. New York: Thames & Hudson, 2000.

Williams, Ronald. "A People Come Out of Egypt: An Egyptologist Looks at the Old Testament." In *Congress Volume: Edinburgh 1974*, 231–52. VTSup 28. Leiden: Brill, 1975.

———. *Williams' Hebrew Syntax*. Toronto: University of Toronto Press, 2007.

Wilson, John A. "The God and His Unknown Name of Power." In *Ancient Near Eastern Texts Relating to the Old Testament*, edited by James B. Pritchard, 12–13. Princeton: Princeton University Press, 1969.

Wilson, Robert. "Foreign Words in the Old Testament as an Evidence of Historicity." *PTR* 26 (1928) 177–247.

Wilson, Stephen. *Luke and the Law*. SNTSMS 50. Cambridge: Cambridge University Press, 1983.

Whybray, Norman. *Introduction to the Pentateuch*. Grand Rapids: Eerdmans, 1995.

Wolf, Umhau. "Moses in Christian and Islamic Tradition." *JBR* 27 (1957) 102–8.

Wolfson, Elliot. "Circumcision and the Divine Name: A Study in the Transmission of Esoteric Doctrine." *JQR* 78 (1987) 77–112.

Zurawski, Jason. "Mosaic Paideia." *JSJ* 48 (2017) 480–505.

www.ingramcontent.com/pod-product-compliance
Lightning Source LLC
Chambersburg PA
CBHW051107160426
43193CB00010B/1357